RUTA DEL MODERNISME

Ajuntament de Barcelona

Institut del Paisatge Urbà
i la Qualitat de Vida

HONORARY PATRONS OF THE
BARCELONA MODERNISME ROUTE

El Corte Inglés

EL MUNDO
CATALUNYA

COUNCIL OF HONOUR OF THE BARCELONA MODERNISME ROUTE

Casa Àsia (Palau del Baró de Quadras)

Casa Batlló, SL

Casa-Museu Gaudí

Consell Català de l'Esport (Casa Pere Company)

Delegació del Govern a Catalunya (Palau Montaner)

Fundació Antoni Tàpies

Fundació Caixa Catalunya (Casa Milà, la Pedrera)

Fundació "la Caixa" (CaixaForum - Fàbrica Casaramona, Casa Macaya i CosmoCaixa - Museu de la Ciència)

Fundació Orfeó Català Palau de la Música

Hospital de la Santa Creu i Sant Pau

Institut Amatller d'Art Hispànic (Casa Amatller)

Institut de Cultura de Barcelona (Museu de Zoologia)

Junta Constructora del Temple Expiatori de la Sagrada Família

Museu Nacional d'Art de Catalunya (MNAC)

Parc d'Atraccions Tibidabo, SA (PATSA)

Reial Acadèmia de Ciències i Arts de Barcelona (RACAB) (Observatori Fabra)

Transports Metropolitans de Barcelona, SA (Tramvia Blau)

Turisme de Barcelona (Walking Tours)

Universitat de Barcelona (Pavellons Güell)

CRÈDITS

Published by: Institut Municipal del Paisatge Urbà i la Qualitat de Vida (IMPUiQV), Ajuntament de Barcelona
Av. Drassanes, 6-8, planta 21. 08001 Barcelona.
Tel: +34 932 562 509
cultura-impuqv@mail.bcn.es
www.paisatgeurba.com

President: Jordi Portabella

Manager: Ricard Barrera

Routes and Publishing Department:
Lluís Bosch (Department head)
Jordi París (Modernisme Route co-ordinator)
Armando Gonzàlez (design and logistics)
Pep Ferré
Inma Pascual
Sònia Turon

Barcelona Modernisme Route
Second period, first edition, June 2005

Texts:
Modernisme, Between Love and Hate: Josep M. Huertas
Barcelona Modernisme Route: Antoni Capilla
Guapos per sempre: Mònica Maspoch
Beyond Barcelona: Joan Bassegoda, Victòria Claver, Carme Clusellas, Isabel Coll, Consorci de la Colònia Güell, Domènech Ferran, Oficina de Turisme de Manresa, Dominique Ruiz and Pilar Vera Sanromà.

Photographs: David Aasen, Ajuntament d'Esplugues del Llobregat, Arxiu Històric de la Ciutat (AHCB-AF), Arxiu PMTC, Miquel Badia, Xavier Bolao, Marc Bosch de Dòria, Jordi Buxó, Casa Batlló (Pere Vivas and Ricard Pla), Lluís Casals, Consorci de la Colònia Güell, Consorci del Patrimoni de Sitges, Joan Anton Fontanals, Domènec Freixedes, Sheila Garcia, Josep Grifoll, Carlos Iglesias, IMPUiQV, Institut Municipal de Museus de Reus, Joan Iriarte, Junta Constructora Temple Sagrada Família, Llibreria Millà, Teresa Llordés, Adolf Mas - Institut Amatller d'Art Hispànic, Museu Arxiu Tomàs Balvey, Museu Nacional d'Art de Catalunya - MNAC (Jordi Calveras, Marta Mérida and Joan Sagristà), Patronat Municipal de Turisme de Sitges, Salvador Redó, Joan Ribera, Marc Rosés, Oriol Vila and Pedro Zapata.

Cover photo: inside the Sagrada Familia Temple. (c) Carlos Iglesias

Design: Tcrea Diseño Integral, SL; José Maria Olivella, Mònica Pujol, Laura Garcia

Translation: Tau Traduccions, SL and IMPUiQV.

Printed by: Gramagraf, SCCL

Acknowledgements: Centre de Normalització Lingüística de Barcelona and Cercle del Liceu

ISBN: 84-934169-4-0
DL: B-17.746-2005

Printed in Catalonia

ACKNOWLEDGEMENTS

Marta Aladrén, Santiago Alcolea, Roser Alegre, Eulàlia Almuzara, Francisco Alonso, Alexandre Amat, Gemma Armengol, Esteve Barandica, Ángel Barón, Dolors Bas, Joan Bassegoda, Mercedes Basso, Encarna Bayona, Núria Benet, Nina Bernat, Elionor Bertran, Anna Biosca, Gemma Bladé, Ariadna Blanch, Montserrat Blanch, Bofarull family, Sacramento Broceño, Magda Brusau, Josep M. Cabré, Tate Cabré, Johanna Càceres, Oriol Calvo, Mariana Campillo, Marta Canals, Marc Capella, Andreu Carrascal, Josep Castelló, Salvador Claramunt, Victòria Claver, Carme Cluselles, Anna Coll, Ivan Condés, Mònica Cosials, Mònica Cruz, Curro, Mercè Curull, Eulàlia Dalmau, Lluïsa Daniel, Imma Domènech, Miquel Domènech, Rosa Dòria, Jordi Eduardo, Aurelia Escalante, Domènec Ferran, Ivan Ferré, Lourdes Figueras, Eduard Fornés, Nuria Fradera, Serena Fracanzani, Mireia Freixa, Cristina Gabarró, Jaime Garcia, Rosa Garicano, Josep Maria Garrut, Joan Bautista Gené, Núria Gil, J.L. Giménez -Frontín, Montserrat Giralt, Alicia Gómez, Lluís Gómez, Arantxa González, Granada family, Agustí Grau, Mariona Grau, Gemma Griñó, Mònica Guerrero, Guilera family, Carme Guinea, Ramon Gurruchaga, M. Antònia Hernàndez, Herrero family, Esperanza Holgado, M. Àngels Isern, Josep Jornet, Cristina Langarika, Gemma Llobet, Carmen Maciel, Paz Madorrán, Antonio Magaña, Joaquín Marquina, Yolanda Martín, Teresa Martínez , Francesc Masip, Anna M. Mata, Fabià Matas, Maria Mena, Cristina Mendoza, Laura Mercader, Ricard Mestre, Michael, Blanca Moll, Alícia Montes, Abraham del Moral, Antoni Moreno, Isabel Moreno, Joan Mulet, Anna Omedes, Pilar Oyaga, Carlos de Pablo Pérez, Elisabet Pagés, Bárbara Palacios, Juan Carlos Parellada, Vinyet Parés, Alejandra de la Paz, Sylvia Pederzini, Glòria Peiró, Guillem Peiró, Anna Perarnau, Abel Pérez, Montse Pérez, Malú Piedrabuena, Pere Pina, Mar Prat, Patrícia Prats, Frederic Prieto, Jaume de Puig, Núria Ransanz, Quim Ribot, Cristina Rivas, Manuel Rodríguez, M. Àngels Rodulfo, Judith Roig, Gemma Roma, Josep M. Rosés, Dominique Ruiz, Núria Ruiz , Josep Sales, Pilar Salmerón, Antoni Sampere, José Maria Sànchez, Victor Sànchez, Romina Sans, Sònia Sarmiento, Eloisa Sendra, Pepe Serra, Raúl Serra, Santiago Siquier, Ramon Solé, Alex Susanna, Mònica Terol, Mariona Teruel, Tutusaus family, Anna Valls, Victòria Valls, Montserrat Vázquez, Pilar Vera, Eduard Vidal, Yolanda Vilar, Silvia Vilarroya, Laia Vinaixa, Daniel Zafra.

Special thanks to the personnel of the Institut del Paisatge Urbà i la Qualitat de Vida and of the Ajuntament de Barcelona for their enthusiastic support to the Barcelona Modernisme Routc projcct.

How to Use this Guide

This book will guide you along the Modernisme Route, which includes up to one-hundred and fifteen works considered to be the most relevant in Barcelona.

As you are walking through the city's landscape, you will also be guided by the red round tiles that are set in the street pavement. These tiles show the general direction in the main sections of the Route (the One-day route), passing in front of the Modernista buildings. In the other sections and in detours, however, you will find only one tile in front of each Modernista building.

To help you organise your discovery of the Barcelona's Modernista heritage, the guide is structured as a single recommended walk, with detours to reach all the monuments. It may take from four days to one week to complete the whole route, depending on the time spent on visiting each building.

For a quick introduction, the Modernisme Route recommends the Barcelona Walking Tours, organised by Turisme de Barcelona, a two-hour tour starting from the tourist bureau in Plaça Catalunya.

If you have only one day, this guide offers the **One-day route**, which bypasses all the detours. It can be completed comfortably on foot in one day, and still leaves time for one full visit inside a building. We recommend that you do the whole walk first and then return to the building of your choice to go inside, particularly in winter to make full use of daylight. The One-day route is marked on the maps with a green line, which represents the backbone of Barcelonan Modernisme: la Rambla, Passeig de Gràcia, Avinguda Diagonal, and Avinguda Gaudí. To follow the text of the guide while walking along this direct route, a green icon on the margin of the page marks where each of the sections of the One-day route start. When the text comes to a detour, the paragraph ends with the negative image of the same icon , and tells you the page in which the One-day route continues.

If you prefer to set your own pace and discover the best masterpieces each at a time, **30 highly recommended buildings** have been selected out of the Route's 111. These "Star Monuments" of the Route have been marked ☆ in the Contents section of the guide. The Modernisme Route discount vouchers (see the last page of this guide) are valid for one whole year to allow you to visit all the buildings open to the public at your leisure.

The *"Forever Beautiful"* chapter contains a selection of Modernista shops and other public establishments: they are renowned not only for their marvellous decoration, but also for the quality of their products and service.

And once you have had your fill of Barcelona's beautiful architecture, there is still much to see: the "Beyond Barcelona" chapter of the guide invites you to visit other Catalan towns to discover their astounding Modernista treasures.

Please notice: opening hours of parks, buildings and museums may vary with the seasons along the year. It is advised to check them in advance.

For further information visit our website **www.rutadelmodernisme.com**, or contact our Modernisme Centres, where you can obtain the Route map and discount vouchers.

Key to the *Barcelona Modernisme Route* guide and maps:

1 **CASA ESTAPÉ (1)**
Building or element of the Route. The number helps to locate it on the map

ARC DE TRIOMF
Interesting building or element which is not Modernista

The One-day Route is marked by a green line on the map. In the text you may follow it with:

Point in the text where the One-day route starts or continues after a detour.

-› page 34
Point in the text where a detour begins, and page in which the One-day route continues: until that page, the text will follow the detour.

☆ "Star monument": one of the thirty most recommended buildings of the Route.

Contents

Foreword

In the early 20th century the grid plan that Ildefons Cerdà designed for the Eixample of Barcelona was occupied by buildings of unusual exuberance, the like of which had never been seen before. Figures such as Puig i Cadafalch, Domènech i Montaner and Gaudí introduced an architecture that was not understood so much as a trade but as an art form and, as such, had to innovate and join the new trends of the time. This was how, in a short time, Barcelona acquired an exceptional Modernista heritage and became a city in which the best monuments are the buildings themselves.

A few years later, however, with the arrival of Noucentisme (a far more austere movement) Modernisme came to be considered an almost unforgivable extravagance. In his book *Barcelona Modernista*, Eduardo Mendoza recalls how some tourist guides to the city of the twenties and thirties apologised for the strange and horrible buildings that occupied the city. This attitude resulted in the loss, for example, of the magnificent sculptures that decorated the facade of the Casa Lleó Morera, which was one of the outstanding models in the exhibition "Cities, Corners" of the 2004 Universal Forum of Cultures in Barcelona.

Fortunately, the city has managed to recover its Modernista heritage through restoration work and ambitious maintenance projects for buildings, to the point that Modernisme has become one of its main attractions. The City Council has made a great effort towards achieving this aim, through actions such as the exhibition "El Quadrat d'Or" in 1990 and the introduction in 1997 of the Modernisme Route, with which we wish to offer the people of Barcelona, and also the visitors to the city, an original way of discovering this heritage.

The Modernisme Route is a collective project involving all the entities directly related to the Modernista heritage. It devotes its profits totally to the protection and promotion of this impressive architectural heritage.

In order to further promote this heritage we have created the new guide of the Barcelona Modernisme Route that you are now holding, a book with which we wish to invite you to walk around the city and admire the genius of a group of architects who understood the need to seek new, more dynamic forms that were able to combine the different fields of the arts.

Joan Clos i Mateu

Mayor of Barcelona

Foreword

In the 21st century the city of Barcelona is universally known and recognised for the unique quality of its Modernista heritage. Called by some "the Mecca of Modernisme", our city is definitely an unquestionable point of reference for international art. This has not always been the case, and today it seems strange to recall that only thirty years ago Gaudí was almost unknown by the general public. Time often ends up putting things in their right place, but this would be too simplistic an explanation of how Barcelona's Modernisme has grown out of oblivion to be the highly popular cultural phenomenon it is today.

This spectacular progress has been achieved during the last 25 years thanks to the collective effort of a whole city. The first democratic City Council of 1979 already had a clear intention of protecting the Modernista heritage, and after the tremendous success of International Gaudí Year in 2002 this is still an important objective. However, the City Council has always been fully aware that without the spirit of enterprise of our institutions, companies and entities, and of the thousands of small owners and shopkeepers, Barcelona would not today have the magnificent display of architectural brilliance and craftsmanship left to us by our great-grandparents. It has been the result of three decades of pioneering research, rigorous restoration and careful maintenance. Furthermore, some exemplary projects of cultural management have been set up, and they have proved that Modernisme can be very attractive for tourists without falling into simplification and vulgarity.

Since 1997, the Modernisme Route of Barcelona City Council has been part of this collective effort, offering citizens and visitors an original, versatile and advantageous way of discovering our Modernisme. It is also important to note that the Route is more than this new, extended and improved edition of the guide which you are now holding. The Barcelona Modernisme Route is a endeavour of the City Council to foster Modernisme through the involvement of the organisations that are most related to it. This is why the profits from the sales of this guide are devoted totally to the preservation and promotion of Barcelona's Modernisme. With this in mind, exploring and discovering this magnificent heritage with your Barcelona Modernisme Route guide may be even more pleasant.

Jordi Portabella i Calvete

Second Deputy Mayor of Barcelona

President of the Institut del Paisatge Urbà i la Qualitat de Vida

Modernisme, between Love and Hate

Josep M. Huertas Claveria

The art critic Francesc Fontbona is right in believing that Modernisme has gradually become "a kind of magic word within Catalan culture," and that "there are those who, without wishing to, have given it a special charisma as a patriotic emblem that is totally excessive and out of all proportion" (1). This has not, however, always been the case, and one might be surprised to read articles of judicious people such as Carles Soldevila, Josep Plà and Manuel Brunet, for example, calling for the demolition of the Palau de la Música because they considered it to be an architectural aberration. This example is the tip of the iceberg of clearly anti-Modernista way of thinking that had a decisive influence on Catalan thought between the twenties and the fifties.

Amidst the love-hate relations that have been unleashed in the course of the time, Modernisme has a history that is not always easy to date.

THE EIGHTIES

Alexandre Cirici Pellicer, a highly proficient historian and art critic, set the beginning of Modernisme in Catalonia in the period 1880-85, when five buildings as different as Casa Vicens, by Antoni Gaudí; the Víctor Balaguer museum-library in Vilanova i la Geltrú, by Jeroni Granell i Mundet the Academy of Sciences in the Rambla of Barcelona, by Josep Domènech i Estapà; the no longer existing Indústries d'Art de Francesc Vidal by Josep Vilaseca, and the Montaner i Simón publishing firm —today Fundació Tàpies— by Lluís Domènech i Montaner.

As the architect Oriol Bohigas states in a text in defence of Modernisme, this artistic movement "has such an extraordinary projection and intensity in Catalonia, and takes on at least such a sharp and transcendental personality as that of the foreign movements that were to some extent parallel, such as Liberty, Secession, Art Nouveau, Jugendstil or the Modern Style (2)."

Modernisme sought modernity on the one hand and cultural regeneration on the other. A group of intellectuals whose core was the editorial staff of the weekly magazine *L'Avens* gave the movement content. They did not merely promote architecture, the cornerstone of Modernisme, but also the sculpture, painting, graphic arts, literature, theatre and the recovery of the traditional craft trades which were so skilfully used by the great architects.

The phenomenon came to an end between 1910 and 1914, according to Professor Joaquim Molas, in 1911 according to Oriol Bohigas, and between 1909 and 1910 according to the art historian Mireia Freixa. Whatever the case may be, it is clear that it was present in Catalan cultural life for about thirty years, though some late examples, such as the Casa Planells by Josep Maria Jujol (1923-24), are considered to be Modernista masterpieces.

View of Ålesund

BRUSSELS, VIENNA, ALESUND

When one travels to a city that also had its Art Nouveau period, it is easy to establish comparisons, though the styles are highly different. The Viennese Secession has a more distinct personality, but some houses of the Brussels Art Nouveau could be transported to the urban landscape of Barcelona. An interesting case is the port town of Alesund in Norway, which was destroyed by fire in the early 20th century. It was rebuilt in only three years, from 1904 to 1907, and this gave it a unique profile as an example of Jugendstil in the world. The period of this reconstruction coincides with that of maximum splendour of Catalan Modernisme, the first decade of the 20th century.

THE PROMOTERS

The men and women who made Modernisme possible formed part of a privileged social group of manufacturers, investors, bankers and new nobility who had become rich in the late 19th century, according to Dolors Llopart(3). A factor that contributed to this was the repatriation of capital from Cuba after the loss of Spain's last colonies.

For this upwardly mobile bourgeoisie, the clearest sign of distinction was to commission the construction of a new building in the Eixample, an expansion area of Barcelona that was being developed at that time. The admiration or envy caused by an unusual house,

Josep Llimona, 1907 - *Desconsol*

such as that of the Batlló family, redesigned by Antoni Gaudí, led Pere Milà to ask the same architect to build another one in Passeig de Gràcia, which became Casa Milà, known as La Pedrera. The institutions also wished to construct outstanding buildings in Modernista style, such as the Hospital de Sant Pau by Domènech i Montaner and the Sagrada Família by Gaudí.

Sculptors such as Josep Llimona, Miquel Blay and Enric Clarasó excelled in their Modernista statues. *Desconsol* by Llimona in the former Arms Yard of Parc de la Ciutadella, and *La cançó popular*, by Miquel Blay, on the corner of Palau de la Música's façade, are two of the most representative sculptures of this phenomenon, but not the only ones. Montjuïc and Poblenou cemeteries, for instance, have a remarkable parade of Modernista sculptures.

Painters such as Ramon Casas and Santiago Rusiñol were the main exponents of Modernisme in their art, and the cafe Els Quatre Gats, located on the ground floor

Ramon Casas, 1897 - ***Ramon Casas i Pere Romeu on a tandem***

of Casa Martí by Puig i Cadafalch, was a meeting point for those who placed their faith in the dictates of the new art form. Even some posters by Picasso can be considered to be Modernista, alongside the better known ones by Alexandre de Riquer and Adrià Gual.

In addition to the posters, there were the covers of some books printed by publishers such as Montaner i Simón, and periodicals such as *Pèl & Ploma, Joventut, Hispania and Garba*. In literature, *Els sots ferèstecs*, by Raimon Casellas, and *Solitud*, by Víctor Català, were two of the most important works of literary Modernisme. The performance in Sitges, in 1897, of *La fada*, a play by Jaume Massó i Torrents, director of the weekly magazine *L'Avens*, was a special moment in Symbolist theatre, which went hand in hand with Modernisme.

Pujol i Bausis ceramics factory

Lluís Domènech i Montaner, 1905, Casa Lleó Morera - Glasswork by Rigalt Granell i Cia

THE MINOR ARTS

The concept of a minor art is certainly mistaken, but it has been used for so long that it allows us to understand each other. Joan Busquets is one of the major exponents of this excellent period of recovery of craftsmanship. He came from a dynasty of carpenters and created some of the most highly appreciated Modernista furniture of the time. He and the Majorcan Gaspar Homar were the most important figures in furniture. It would be difficult not to include in the values of Modernisme the famous stained glass work.

A work such as the stained glass windows of the Casa Lleó Morera, by Antoni Rigalt's workshop, is one of the best examples of the applied arts of the time. Other important works are the cast iron produced by the Manyach workshop, the ceramics of the Pujol i Bausis factory, the mosaics of the Escofet company, the jewellery of Lluís Masriera, and the terracotta work of Lambert Escaler.

The spread of Modernisme took place around the turn of the century, probably due to the impact of the Paris Exhibition of 1900, and also because at prosperous time in the economy, the Catalan bourgeoisie felt the need to give their dwellings personality. It was like a social triumph, and magazines such as *Il·lustració Catalana* published examples of the new houses of the bourgeoisie as positive new features of urban development.

Another aspect that is not always mentioned, but that was important in daily life, is the introduction of domestic improvements such as baths and washbasins, in addition to the use of tiles in kitchens and the spread of the use of laundry rooms. Not all have the beauty of the attic in Gaudí's la Pedrera, but hygiene and comfort benefited from the advances proposed by many Modernista architects.

DECADENCE AND DEFENCE

Noucentisme took a hard line with Modernisme, from which it took over. It considered the more extravagant examples of the former movement to be in poor taste, and many shops and establishments were transformed and decorated in a more austere, discreet and frankly boring style. We still have the photographs that show us what the Diorama Cinema and the Cafè Torino looked like, to mention but two of the many works that were forever lost.

For years not even Gaudí was spared the general scorn, and time had to pass before he was again appreciated. Alexandre Cirici wrote in 1948: "When we ask the people who promoted it about Modernisme, except on rare occasions we are given the evasive answers of shame, a kind of repentance that wishes to bury the past. When we speak with members of the generation under the age of 30, however, we often find a great appreciation and interest in it (4)."

Few texts are more revealing of the post-war period, when Modernisme gradually began to be reconsidered. However, this did not prevent the demolition of Puig i Cadafalch's beautiful Casa Trinxet in 1968, and struggle was necessary to prevent the same from happening to Casa Serra, also by Puig i Cadafalch, and Can Golferics, by Joan Rubió i Bellvé.

In 1968, with a major exhibition and the publication of *Arquitectura modernista*, by Oriol Bohigas and Leopold Pomès, the situation began to change and the interest noted by Cirici as a sign of the new generations paved the way for the recovery of a genuinely Catalan artistic movement. Modernisme had aroused love and hate that had to be overcome in order to contemplate it as it is, a great moment of artistic and ideological creation.

NOTES

(1) - FONTBONA, Francesc. "Va existir realment el Modernisme?" In: ***El Modernisme***, p. 45. Lunwerg, 1990.

(2) - BOHIGAS, Oriol. ***Arquitectura modernista***. P. 225. Lumen, 1968.

(3) - LLOPART, Dolors. "De la forma i de l'ús dels objectes". In: ***El Modernisme***, p. 241. Lunwerg, 1990.

(4) - CIRICI, Alexandre. "El Modernisme vist ara". In: ***Ariel***, No. 18. p. 61. Published in 1948

The disappeared Cafè Torino

Barcelona Modernisme Route

In the late 19th century, at the time of the Universal Exhibition of 1888, Barcelona was a bustling city in which architecture played a major role as an indicator of the social status of the then flourishing bourgeoisie. Having a Modernista house meant that one was keeping up with the trends of the social elite. To meet the expectations and vanities of their clients, the architects used their whole repertoire of resources in their work: floral decorations, rich sculptural and wrought iron work, undulating forms, stained glass, sgraffito work, and ceramic details. Large cities can often be associated with buildings and monuments that become their universal emblems. This, however, is not the specific case of Barcelona. The architectural personality of Barcelona is characterised more by its urban landscape than by outstanding individual buildings. One of the areas in which this urban landscape is most exceptional is the Eixample, a district in which there occurred an extraordinary architectural phenomenon at the turn of the century: Modernisme, the particular local version of Art Nouveau, a European trend that led to an outburst of creative activity and also left remarkable architecture in other cities such as Vienna, Munich, Nancy, Brussels, Glasgow or Berlin. This guide will take you on a tour of this phenomenon in Barcelona.

Arc de Triomf

A good place to start the Barcelona Modernisme Route is the **ARC DE TRIOMF** (TRIUMPHAL ARCH. Passeig de Lluís Companys, s/n), built in 1888 at the top of Passeig de Lluís Companys to a design by Josep Vilaseca, which presided over the entrance to the 1888 Exhibition.

The one-day Route starts here. Although this walking tour does not visit all of the most recommended Modernista monuments, it gives a wide, in-depth view of this

Casa Estapé

architecture and is a good option to discover the city in general. This guide will lead you around if you follow the icons on the text margin and the green line on the map.

Before continuing the route down to the Parc de la Ciutadella, you can make a slight
1 detour up Passeig de Sant Joan to **CASA ESTAPÉ** (ESTAPÉ HOUSE. Passeig de Sant Joan, 6) by Bernardí Martorell i Rius (1907), which is easily recognised by its curious dome by Jaume Bernades. Nearby the Arch, on the short Avinguda de Vilanova, you can
☆ 2 see the building of **HIDROELÈCTRICA** (Avinguda de Vilanova, 12), a Modernista building of the former Central Catalana d'Electricitat built by Pere Falqués i Urpí between 1896 and 1899, which can sometimes be visited during office hours.

Hidroelèctrica

Continue down Passeig de Lluís Companys to the **PARC DE LA CIUTADELLA** (CITADEL PARK. Passeig de Pujades, s/n, Passeig de Picasso, s/n). This park can be considered to be the first great architectural expression of the Modernista movement. As its name indicates, the site had formerly been occupied by a military citadel, built in the early 18th century after the defeat of Barcelona in the War of Succession. The city was severely punished when it fell after a long siege, and the Citadel (together with the new walls and Montjuïc castle) was used by the Bourbon dynasty to keep the city under military control for over 150 years. In the mid-19th century, after years of petitioning by the citizens, the government in Madrid agreed to allow the walls and the Citadel to be demolished to make room for the urban development of the city. This made it possible to create the Eixample ("Enlargement") and the new Citadel Park.

General view of the 1888 Universal Exhibition

Before the park was built, however, the land was used as the site for the 1888 Universal Exhibition. Though it was definitely less important than other similar exhibitions, such as those of Paris and London, like them it aimed to reveal the marvels of the new technologies of the incipient capitalist industry, and to make Barcelona known worldwide.

The pavilions and the infrastructures were built rapidly and with a great deal of improvisation. Experienced architects such as Josep Fontserè worked alongside young graduates such as Lluís Domènech i Montaner, who demonstrated his impressive talent for management and coordination, especially in the Gran Hotel Internacional (no longer standing), a building with a capacity for 500 guests which Domènech's team built in less than 60 days. Legend also created many myths and rumours about the role played by Antoni Gaudí in the construction of the Parc de la Ciutadella. Some claim that he collaborated with Josep Fontserè in the building of the waterfall and perhaps also the cistern on Carrer Wellington. Others see Gaudí's mark on the railings of the main gate of the park, and the disappeared pavilion of the Companyia Transatlàntica.

Though the park itself is not considered to be a Modernista garden, it contains some outstanding works in this style. Just beside one of the side doors of the park, in Passeig de Pujades, is the building that was destined to be the Café-Restaurant of the Universal Exhibition. It was built between 1887 and 1888 by Lluís Domènech i Montaner in exposed brickwork, an unusual technique at the time, and is one of the first examples of Barcelona Modernisme. Its crenellated wall, its frieze of coats of arms and its sobriety give it a certain medieval appearance, which is highlighted by the eclectic combination of Catalan arches, large Roman windows and Arabic arches. Since 1920 the building, popularly known as the **CASTELL DELS TRES DRAGONS**

Museu de Zoologia

Castell dels Tres Dragons - Museu de Zoologia

Address	Passeig de Picasso, s/n. Parc de la Ciutadella.
Open	Tuesday to Sunday, 10am to 2.30pm. Thursdays until 6.30pm. Closed on some public holidays
Information	Tel.: 933 196 912. www.bcn.es/museuciencies
Further details	Timetables may change, it is advised to check beforehand. Check updates and information on Route discount at **www.rutadelmodernisme.com** or call 902 076 621.

☆ 3 (Castle of the Three Dragons), has housed the **MUSEU DE ZOOLOGIA** (MUSEUM OF ZOOLOGY) which, together with the Geology Museum, forms the Natural Science Museum. The Castell dels tres Dragons houses the zoology collection and permanent exhibition, and the temporary exhibition rooms of the Natural Science Museum, presided over by a magnificent skeleton of a whale. The building was recently restored respecting the architectural values of the construction and furniture. Nearby are two delightful buildings,
4 the **HIVERNACLE** (GREENHOUSE. Passeig de Picasso, s/n. Parc de la Ciutadella), a work by Josep Amargós i Samaranch (1883-1887) that is currently used for all types of social event,
5 and the **UMBRACLE** (SHADE HOUSE. Passeig de Picasso, s/n. Parc de la Ciutadella), built by Josep Fontserè i Mestres in 1883-1884. It is certainly worth sparing a few minutes to have a look inside both of them and walk around the splendid collection of plants they protect.

Hivernacle

From the Parc de la Ciutadella, walk into the old city centre along Carrer Fusina or Carrer de la Ribera, which will take you to the **MERCAT DEL BORN** (BORN MARKET. Plaça Comercial, 12), until the 1970s the main wholesale market of the city. This structure of iron, wood and glass designed by Josep Fontserè and built in 1876 is an excellent example of the architectural forerunners of Modernisme, which excelled in the design of new structures made possible by using new industrial materials, and in the importance given to natural light. Inside are the ruins discovered in 2001, which are part of the

Umbracle

buildings of the old Barcelona that were demolished to make way for the military Citadel in 1715. These ruins are sometimes open to the public and are part of the History Museum of the City of Barcelona (for more information, call 933 190 222).

Right opposite the market, Passeig del Born, perhaps the only street in Barcelona that is still fully paved in cobblestones characteristic of the first half of the twentieth century. All along this part of the walk we will come across some of the oldest streets of Barcelona, some of them opening under vaults in a medieval style, with names that in many cases refer to the old crafts guilds that grouped together in each one. Passeig del Born will lead you to the **BASÍLICA DE SANTA MARIA DEL MAR** (THE HOLY MARY OF THE SEA'S BASILICA. Plaça de Santa Maria, s/n), dating from the 14th century and one of the most important Catalan Gothic churches. If you go round the building on Carrer Santa Maria you will come to the **FOSSAR DE LES MORERES** (MULBERRY TREE GRAVEYARD. Plaça del Fossar de les Moreres, s/n), one of the main symbols of Catalan nationalism. According to tradition here lie those who died defending Barcelona in the siege of 1714, which was the final episode in the War of Succession in which the European dynasties of Austria and Bourbon fought over the kingdoms of Spain. The memorial placed here in 2001 commemorates this heroic defence of Barcelona by the Catalan militia, who for over a year resisted the alliance of the Spanish and French armies, far superior in number and technology.

On the other side of the Basilica, continue along Carrer Argenteria, cross Via Laietana and go up Carrer Jaume I, which takes you to the heart of the city, the Plaça de Sant Jaume. This square has been the political and administrative centre of the city since mediaeval times: on the right is the Renaissance façade of the Generalitat de Catalunya,

Bar Molly's Fair City

the Catalan autonomous government, while on the left is the Barcelona City Council or Ajuntament, its neoclassical façade hiding a Gothic interior. Just after the square you can turn left into Carrer del Pas de l'Ensenyança to visit the cocktail bar **El Paraigua**, decorated with original Modernista elements salvaged from another establishment. Carrer Ferran will take you to an Irish pub, **MOLLY'S FAIR CITY** (Ferran, 7-9), which was previously a shop and still has much of the original Modernista decoration on both the outside and the inside (for further information see *Let's Go Out*, the guide to Modernista bars and restaurants). Just opposite this pub is the entrance to Plaça Reial, one of the busiest places in the city, with a considerable range of bars and night clubs. This square was the first important urban renewal project in 19th-century Barcelona, and occupies the site of the former Santa Madrona Capuchin monastery, which was demolished in the mid-19th century. The design of this urban space, with its characteristic porticos, is the work of the architect and urbanist Francesc Daniel Molina, who was inspired by the French urbanism of the Napoleonic period and conceived it as a residential square formed by buildings of two storeys plus an attic, built over archways. Right in the centre of the square is the Three Graces fountain, and on both sides of it the complex **FANALS** (LAMP-POSTS. Plaça Reial, s/n) with six lamps designed by a young Antoni Gaudí in 1878. 6 7

The two lamp-posts are decorated with the attributes of the god Hermes, the patron of shopkeepers: a caduceus (a messenger's wand with two snakes wound round it)

Gaudí's Plaça Reial lamp-posts

and a winged helmet. Like Plaça Reial, many other places in the historic centre of Barcelona were built on sites formerly occupied by monasteries and churches that were confiscated by the Spanish government and sold to private owners. These measures, which were carried out in 1837 and known as Mendizábal's disentailment, led to the auction of eighty percent of the land owned by the church within the city walls of Barcelona. The disentailment rapidly led to a thorough and long-lasting transformation of the urban landscape of Barcelona. There are many examples. The Boqueria Market, beside the Rambla, stands on the site occupied successively by the monastery of Santa Maria de Jerusalem (14th century) and the monastery of Sant Josep (16th century). The Gothic convent of Santa Caterina, which was destroyed by fire in 1835 and demolished two years later, lent its site and name to a market that has now been thoroughly remodelled and reconstructed. Even the Liceu Opera House was built on the site of a former Discalced Trinitarian monastery. The other great centre of music of Barcelona, the Palau de la Música Catalana, was built on the ruins of the monastery of Sant Francesc de Paula.

Here we may take a small detour to number 8 of Carrer Escudillers, in order to see the **Grill Room**, an old Modernista restaurant and cafe (for more information, see *Let's go out*, the guide to Modernista bars and restaurants.")

On leaving the square you will come to La Rambla, the famous main artery of Barcelona life. At the time of maximum splendour of the Modernista movement, little development land was available in the old part of Barcelona. Therefore, with the exception of a few shops in the Modernista style, there are few examples in this area of the city. However, ☆ 8 these include masterpieces such as the **PALAU GÜELL** (GÜELL PALACE. Nou de la Rambla, 3-5), the first work (1885-1889) that Antoni Gaudí, the most peculiar and striking architect of the Modernista movement, would offer the city of Barcelona, and now listed World Heritage by UNESCO. Gaudí was only 34 years old when he received the commission to build the private residence of the Güell family. And curiously it was not in the Eixample, which was already in full expansion, but in the Raval, a degraded zone that in the late 19th century had been taken over by prostitution and was full of brothels. Perhaps it was not very logical that Eusebi Güell, with seven children, should choose

Palau Güell

Address	Nou de la Rambla, 3-5
Open	Closed to the public for restoration works until january 2007
Information	Tel.: 933 173 974 and www.diba.es/palauguell/index.htm També al lloc web: **www.rutadelmodernisme.com** or call 902 076 621.

to live there, but he had a reason for doing so. His father, Joan Güell, lived in the Rambla and Eusebi bought the site of the Palau Güell to be near him. Gaudí's aristocratic patron gave the architect a free budget to build a sumptuous, original palace in which to hold political meetings and chamber music concerts and to accommodate the most illustrious guests of the family. No sooner said than done. Gaudí used the best materials of the time and the construction costs soared. The final result was a masterpiece in Gaudí's darkest style. Far from satisfying the bourgeois idea of comfort (it is a very tall building which was then without heating, so it must have been rather uncomfortable in winter), Gaudí's Palau Güell is an unusual space featuring a magnificent, skilfully crafted interplay of volumes and light.

The façade of the Palau Güell, with evocative Venetian lines, is built with a stone of severe appearance, which highlights the wrought iron design covering the tympana

Palau Güell - Main entrance

of the two parabolic entrance and exit arches and forming the majestic coat of arms with the Catalan emblem, conceived as a small colonnade. The first area of the palace is the 20 metre-high foyer that gives the building a transparent appearance and articulates the different spaces into which this magnificent early work by Gaudí is divided. The whole building is organised around the central foyer. A majestic staircase leads to the authentic jewel in the crown of the Palau Güell: its surprising, mysterious, telluric central hall rising seven stories and crowned by a parabolic,

Palau Güell

cone-shaped dome. The dome is perforated by a series of small openings arranged in a circle that filter gentle indirect light, giving the hall a curious appearance that some experts liken to a planetarium in daylight and others to the central hall of an *Arab hammam*.

The roof terrace has twenty chimneys designed by Gaudí and restored between 1988 and 1992 by a group of artists who rebuilt the eight that had been most damaged, observing respect for Gaudí's original work (on one of these new chimneys, however, with a little patience one can find Cobi, the Olympic mascot dog of Barcelona '92, depicted among the trencadís). This was the first work in which Gaudí used *trencadís*, a facing technique of Arabic origin using irregular tile fragments, which Gaudí and the Modernista movement adopted as one their characteristic features. The Gaudinian chimneys, all unique and different as if they were different sketches of an idealised model, probably represent one of the first drafts of the design that Gaudí would culminate years later on the roof terrace of La Pedrera. With a little imagination they recall a group of trees. On one of them, which is totally white and was probably the last one built by Gaudí, the small green stamp of a pottery manufacturer of Limoges can be seen. The legend goes that Eusebi Güell had a marvellous dinner service from Limoges that he was tired of, and he gave them to the architect for use in the cladding of the last chimney of the Palau.

The basement is a peculiar crypt of very low vaults supported by simple fungiform columns, a spectacular work of architecture which formerly housed the stables and the grooms' quarters. The brick columns and their capitals form one of the most

Palau Güell - Dining room and basement

Palau Güell - Roof terrace

Antoni Gaudí i Cornet (1852-1926)

Antoni Gaudí i Cornet was born in 1852 in Reus to a family of coppersmiths from Riudoms. The smallest of five brothers, he moved to Barcelona in 1873 to study architecture, which he finished four years later. It is said that on awarding him his degree, the Director of the School of Architecture, Elies Rogent, muttered "Who knows whether we have given the degree to a madman or a genius: only time will tell". His first professional assignment was to design the new buildings of the textile cooperative of Mataró (1878), for which Gaudí conceived unusual catenary arches of wood and a giant bronze bee (symbol of the cooperative). In the same year, he designed a glass and crystal ware cabinet decorated with wrought-iron, mahogany and marquetry for a Catalan glove manufacturer, Esteban Cornellá, to display his products at the Universal Exhibition of Paris. The display cabinet seduced Eusebi Güell, an industrialist, aristocrat and rising politician, who was to become the patron of the young architect. Gaudí's first commission for Güell was to design the furniture of the pantheon that the Marquis of Comillas, Güell's all-powerful father-in-law, possessed on the outskirts of Santander. This assignment was followed by another, a pergola decorated with globes and hundreds of glass pieces. From then on his career and his work, which in the course of time became one of the most famous symbols of Barcelona, were intimately linked to the Güell family.

In 1883 the Church commissioned him to build the Sagrada Família, which was to become the great work of his life, and in which he invested all the efforts of his last years. This gradual concentration on the great expiatory temple ran parallel to the consolidation of a fervent Catholicism, an aspect which had not been apparent in the young Gaudí. In his maturity, the great Catalan architect was known to be a frugal and solitary man who devoted all his energy to the profession through which he expressed his two great passions: Christianity and Catalan nationalism. His obstinate defence of Catalan identity even led to his arrest by the police in 1924 on Catalan National day (11th September), for refusing to submit to an officer who ordered him to speak in Spanish.

On 7th June 1926, Gaudí was hit by a tram when he was crossing the Gran Via. Initially on his admission the staff of the hospital, who struggled to save his life for three days, took him for a beggar because of his humble attire.

enigmatic, evocative and best-known landscapes of Gaudí's architecture. Though it was conceived as a family residence, the Palau Güell was used for this purpose for only a few years. The Güell family lived in it until the Spanish Civil War (1936-39), when the palace was confiscated by the anarchist trade unions CNT-FAI, which turned it into a barracks and prison. The Güells never returned. The general abandon and deterioration of this area of the Raval led the heirs of Count Güell to decide, in 1945, to transfer the palace to the Barcelona Provincial Council, its current owner.

9

Not far from Palau Güell up Carrer Nou de la Rambla is the **LONDON BAR** (Nou de la Rambla, 34), a Modernista bar that has been open for almost a century, since 1910 (for further information see *Let's Go Out*, the guide to Modernista bars and restaurants).

London Bar

The Barcelona Modernisme Route continues up the Rambla towards Plaça de Catalunya. Almost opposite Plaça Reial's porticos is the **HOTEL ORIENTE** (Rambla, 45-47), built in 1842 when the old religious school of Sant Bonaventura was converted into a thriving inn. The hotel, which remodelled its façade in 1881, preserves in its ballroom the magnificent structure of a 17th-century cloister with square pillars and an old rectangular refectory covered with a vault. It has accommodated such distinguished guests as the writer Hans Christian Andersen, the American actor Errol Flynn, the bullfighter Manolete and the soprano Maria Callas. Its discreet façade features the sculptures of two angels standing above the arch of the main entrance.

Gran Teatre del Liceu - Cercle del Liceu

Continuing up the Rambla one comes to one of the most emblematic buildings of the city, though it is not in the Modernista style: the **GRAN TEATRE DEL LICEU** (LICEU OPERA HOUSE. Rambla, 51-65). The history of this emblem of Barcelona has been marked by fire. The original opera house, built by Miquel Garriga in 1847 on the site of a Trinitarian monastery, was burnt down in 1861 and rebuilt by Josep Oriol Mestres. On the exterior, its simplicity is only broken by its characteristic façade with a central body of three large windows, but on the interior it is one of the most lavishly decorated opera houses in the world. After the theatre burnt down again in 1994, it was rebuilt once more, this time by the architect Ignasi de Solà-Morales, who restored it to its original lavish style and recovered the rooms with trompe l'oeil and Pompeiian paintings. In its first period as an opera house, the Liceu had to compete with the **TEATRE PRINCIPAL** (Rambla, 27), which had a capacity for 2,000 persons and a long tradition in the city. The Liceu, which raised the first curtain with *Anna Bolena* by Donizetti, came out the winner, becoming a cathedral of good taste and the favourite showcase for the more opulent classes of Barcelona to display their wealth. Despite the sobriety of its architecture, it features a canopy of wrought iron over the main entrance and sgraffito work that pays homage to Calderón de la Barca, Mozart, Rossini and Moratín. Almost at the corner of the Rambla and Carrer Sant Pau, the building of the Liceu houses a truly elitist sanctuary: the Cercle del Liceu, a traditional and aristocratic private institution, an old club in the purest English style, which conceals in its inner rooms memorable works by the Modernista painters Ramon Casas and Alexandre de Riquer, in addition to stained glass decorated with Wagnerian themes by Oleguer Junyent.

Camiseria Bonet when it was still an outfitter's

On the other side of the street, the route comes to an establishment with a long tradition that has Modernista decoration on the façade, **CAMISERIA BONET** (BONET OUTFITTER'S. Rambla, 72), a former outfitter's shop founded in 1890, which changed ownership in 2002, and now sells mainly Barcelona souvenirs, but has kept its outer decoration virtually untouched. In the adjoining building is the **CAFÈ DE L'ÒPERA** (Rambla, 74), a café with a cosy atmosphere opened in 1929 on the premises of the former La Mallorquina chocolate shop. Featuring inside, the well-preserved original furniture: the Thonet chairs and the nineteenth-century mirrors with female figures suggesting characters from different operas (for further information see *Let's Go Out*, the guide to Modernista bars and restaurants). → page 44 10 11

Café de l'Òpera

After the Liceu, on the left, the route leaves La Rambla momentarily to make a detour down Carrer Sant Pau. The history of hotels in Barcelona would be incomplete without the **HOTEL ESPAÑA** (Sant Pau, 9-11), one of its oldest establishments. The main architectural interest of this hotel, which formerly accommodated the Philippine national hero José Rizal, lies in its public rooms, decorated in 1902-1903 by one of the fathers of Modernisme, Lluís Domènech i Montaner. In the Hotel España, Domènech 12

Hotel España - Painting by R. Casas

i Montaner worked with two great masters of the plastic arts of the time: the sculptor Eusebi Arnau and the painter Ramon Casas. Eusebi Arnau made the splendid alabaster chimney in one of the dining rooms, which is visible from the street, and Ramon Casas did the marine sgraffito work in the interior dining room, which also features a coffered skylight that casts gentle lighting on Casas's work. Domènech i Montaner completed the work with two ingenious wooden wainscots. One of them, of meticulous design, is decorated with blue tiles representing the Spanish provinces, whereas the other, of Roman type, depicts floral themes (for further information see Let's Go Out, the guide to Modernista bars and restaurants). A few steps from the Hotel España there is another hotel with touches of Modernisme: the **HOTEL PENINSULAR** (Sant Pau, 36). The main interest of this building, a former religious school, lies in its court with galleries and a skylight that enhances the green and cream colours of the walls.

13

Hotel Peninsular

Back on La Rambla, the Route comes to Pla de la Boqueria, presided over by the **MOSAIC CERÀMIC DE JOAN MIRÓ** (CERAMIC MOSAIC BY JOAN MIRÓ) placed here by the City Council in 1976, which in the course of time has become an emblematic image of the most popular street in Barcelona. Close by on the right you will find the **CASA BRUNO CUADROS** (BRUNO CUADROS HOUSE. Rambla, 82), a very interesting pre-Modernista building by Josep Vilaseca, the designer the Triumphal Arch of 1888. This ancient house, known popularly as "the Umbrella House", was restored in 1883, incorporating oriental features such as the decoration of the façade with sgraffito work and stained glass, the Egyptian-style gallery on the first floor and the Chinese dragon that protrudes from the corner of the building. The old shop of the building, today occupied by a bank, has ornamental elements of Japanese inspiration in wood, glass and wrought iron.

Many other shops in Barcelona had a similar fate to this one. In 1962, architect David John Mackay estimated that there were 800 Modernista shops in the city. With the passing of time and the relentless work of bulldozers, this number has now been reduced to about fifty. Day by day there are fewer survivors of this Modernisme that some have unjustly called "minor" only because it was smaller in size than the large works of architecture. Some of these shops have been conserved in their full splendour, whereas others survive as best they can in isolated locations of the city. Some are in good condition, others are in a pitiful state, but all have an artistic unity that allows one to reconstruct - surrounded by stucco, mosaic, stained glass and carved mahogany- those years between the Universal Exhibition of 1888 and the second decade of the 20th century. This was a time in which the bourgeoisie of Barcelona travelled to Paris and firmly believed that Catalonia was Europe, a time in which Modernisme became a daily presence and made works of art out of the most vulgar articles. The euphoria of the turn of the century, the desire for renewal, was translated into a social use of art, an anonymous and popular art that dignified any design. It thus came about that baker's shops, cake shops, chemist's, clothiers or perfumeries were treated with the same respect in their decoration as the mansions of the bourgeoisie. In addition to Casa Batlló, La Pedrera, Park Güell and the Sagrada Família, many small establishments wore the new Modernista style with pride. In 1909, the magazine *L'Esquella de la Torratxa* summarised in a single phrase the Modernista fever that was running through the city: "Barcelona is destined to be the Athens of Art Nouveau". A selection of the best examples of Modernista shops still open nowadays can be found in this guide in the chapter *"Forever Beautiful"*.

Casa Doctor Genové

The best example of this Modernista fever that ran through Barcelona is provided by two almost adjoining buildings on the Rambla. **CASA DOCTOR GENOVÉ** 14 (DOCTOR GENOVÉ HOUSE. Rambla, 77) by Enric Sagnier i Villavecchia (1911) housed a chemist's shop and its laboratory until 1974 (now replaced by a Basque tapes

La Rambla

Engraving depicting Barcelona with the Rambla walls still standing, by M. Beaurin (1718)

The original Rambla was a wide, rambling path that ran down the southern limits of the city parallel to the medieval wall built by king James 1st in the 13th century. One hundred years later a new wall would surround the Raval and leave the Rambla wall enclosed, without its theoretical defensive function. However, the wall gates (Santa Anna, Portaferrissa, Boqueria, Trentaclaus and Framenors) did not disappear and continued to be meeting points for open air markets, or were "recycled" into new buildings, such as a cannon factory. "Rambla", in Arabic, means "watercourse" and this is precisely what it was: a torrent, known as the Cagalell, which had become both the sewer and the moat of the city. In the 16th century, the first religious centres (Convent de Sant Josep, 1586), schools (Estudis Generals, 1536) and theatres (Teatro de la Santa Creu, 1597) began to appear on the southern bank. Thus the 17th-century Rambla had the city wall on one side and churches and convents on the other side, in what is now the Raval district. In the late 18th century, military engineers under Juan M. Cermeño transformed this wide ditch into an elegant avenue, channelling the stream under ground and clearing plots for new, aligned buildings.

There is only one Rambla, but each section has been given a different name: going up from the port you will walk along Rambla de Santa Mònica, Rambla dels Caputxins, Rambla de Sant Josep, Rambla dels Estudis and Rambla de Canaletes. These names are not gratuitous but correspond to the monasteries, churches or buildings that stood beside the avenue that began to take shape as the ditch was filled in. In 1768 old king James's wall was demolished and work began on the construction of some of the most emblematic buildings, such as Palau de la Virreina and Palau Moja, which are on the Modernisme Route path, and Casa March de Reus (built by Joan Soler i Faneca in 1780) which is left behind down the Rambla, at number 8. The last great transformation of the Rambla was in the 19th century, when the disentailment of the church's property as a result of liberal policies led to the disappearance of most monasteries that stood on it. They were replaced by new streets (Carrer Ferran), public spaces (Plaça Reial), markets (La Boqueria) and buildings that have become emblematic (Liceu). The Rambla is currently the best showcase of the city, of its history and of the life of its citizens, as was described by the Catalan writer Josep Pla in one of his works: "The Rambla is a marvel. It is one of the few streets of Barcelona in which I feel fully at ease. There are always enough people to meet someone you know, but there are always enough people to go unnoticed if you wish".

bar). Sagnier designed a building with a slightly Gothic appearance featuring a large central window, blue mosaics and a pointed entrance arch, with a magnificent relief of Aesculapius that recalls the original use of the building. Almost next to the former chemist's shop is the **ANTIGA CASA FIGUERAS** (FORMER FIGUERAS HOUSE. Rambla, 83), currently Pastisseria Escribà, a cake shop with an elaborate Modernista decoration by Antoni Ros i Güell (1902), with an abundance of mosaics, stucco, wrought iron, stained glass and wooden furniture in chocolate colour. 15

Antiga Casa Figueras

One does not have to walk too far to find

16 the **MERCAT DE LA BOQUERIA** (BOQUERIA MARKET. Rambla, 91), the oldest and most famous market in the city. From ancient times there had been, more or less in the same place, an open-air market in which the farmers from what is now the Raval district sold their products to the inhabitants of the walled city. Famous for the quality of its merchandise, the market occupies the former site of the Discalced Carmelite monastery of Sant Josep, which was burnt down in July 1835. The market was built five years later, in 1840, as a large porticoed square with Ionic columns under which the travelling tradesmen of the city could offer their varied products. A few years later, in 1914, an attractive metal roof designed by the engineer Miquel de Bergue was added. The market and its surroundings have been restored in recent years to the way they were in the early 20th century. The Boqueria is set in the central section of the Rambla- perhaps the most colourful and exuberant one: the Rambla de les Flors owes its name to the score of flower stalls that have been open all year round since Corpus Christi Day in 1853.

Mercat de la Boqueria

A few steps from the Boqueria one finds the **PALAU DE LA VIRREINA** (VICEREINE'S PALACE. Rambla, 99), built by Josep Ausich in 1778 for the former Viceroy of Peru, Manuel Amat i Junyent. The Viceroy never occupied the building because he died before it was finished. It was, however, occupied by his widow, the Vicereine María Francisca Fivaller, after whom the palace was named in the course of time. It was bought by the City Council in 1944 and in the late 1980s it became the offices of the Municipal Culture Area. The building is a good example of the French influence on architects of the 18th century. The imposing classical façade, sumptuous and Baroque in style, combines perfectly with a French-style Rococo decoration that finds its best example in the vaulted dining room illustrated with allegorical paintings. The remaining rooms in the building still have their original decoration, in Imperial style. The ground floor, which was formerly occupied by the amanuenses who wrote letters for the illiterate, currently houses a bookshop and a citizen's information office. Next to it, on the ground floor of number 97, is the venerated music shop, **CASA BEETHOVEN**, founded in 1880 by the musical publisher Rafael Guàrdia.

Continuing up the Rambla we find one of the most attractive Romantic buildings in the city, **CASA FRANCESC PIÑA** (FRANCESC PIÑA HOUSE. Rambla, 105), also known as

"El Regulador" after the jeweller's shop that occupies the ground floor, today Joieria Bagués. This building by Josep Fontserè (1850) has a terra cotta and white-painted façade with pink stucco work, featuring false columns with capitals and bas-reliefs decorating the upper floors.

At the corner of Carrer del Carme, you will find the **ESGLÉSIA DE BETLEM** (CHURCH OF BETHLEHEM. Rambla, 107), built between 1680 and 1732 by Josep Juli. It is one of the few examples of Baroque art in Barcelona, but in its structure it remains faithful to the precepts of previous Catalan Gothic architecture, with a wide single nave flanked by chapels. Of the doors giving onto the Rambla, one was designed by Francesc Santacruz in 1690 and portrays Christ the Child; the other, portraying Saint John the Baptist, was designed in 1906 by Enric Sagnier taking Santacruz's work as a reference. The church that can be seen today is not as sumptuous as it was before the Civil War of 1936-39, when its polychrome work, carvings, Italian stuccos and marbles were irreparably damaged. Since 1952, the church has kept an image of Our Lady of the Foresaken, by Mariano Benlliure. On the opposite side of the street is the **PALAU MOJA** (MOJA PALACE. Rambla, 118), an old property of the Marquis of Comillas built between 1774 and 1789 by the Mas i Dordal brothers, when the Rambla was transformed into an avenue. The long façade, decorated with ochre and reddish bays, rises above a portico and has a simple central pediment. The building, decorated with paintings by the Neo-Classical painter Francesc Pla, "El Vigatà", still has the original furniture and the room occupied by the catalan "national poet" Jacint Verdaguer, a protégé of the Marquise. The Comillases were related to the Güells, and they also occasionally commissioned works from Gaudí, who thus became acquainted with Verdaguer and even -as in the Pavellons Güell, number **(90)** of the Modernisme Route- used his poetry as an inspiration. The palace currently houses premises of the Culture Department of the Generalitat, the autonomous Catalan government. → page 50

A small detour from the main route leads you up Carrer del Carme, which conceals two Modernista treasures only a few metres from the Rambla: the popular store **EL INDIO** (Carme, 24), decorated in 1922 by Vilaró i Valls in the purest Modernista style, **17**

El Indio

18 and further along, the **BAR MUY BUENAS** (Carme, 63), an establishment with a Modernista façade of wood that still has part of its original furniture, such as the old marble bar, which is over a century old (for further information see *Let's Go Out*, the guide to Modernista bars and restaurants).

Bar Muy Buenas

The route continues up La Rambla, known here as "Rambla dels Ocells" (Rambla of the Birds), because of the stalls selling pets that alternate with the popular newsstands of La Rambla. On the way to Plaça de Catalunya, the route has two
19 important sites. The first is the **REIAL ACADEMIA DE CIÈNCIES I ARTS** (ROYAL ACADEMY OF SCIENCES AND ARTS. Rambla, 115), built in 1883 by Josep Domènech i Estapà on the ruins of a former Jesuit school. In this building the architect was a pioneer in the use of ornamental and stylistic resources that would be such a success years later in the

Reial Acadèmia de Ciències i Arts

Modernista movement. As well as the Reial Acadèmia, the building currently houses the Poliorama Theatre and the Viena restaurant, the former Casa Mumbrú. Its most distinguishing feature is the clock on the façade that is popularly acknowledged to set the official time of Barcelona. Another element of interest on the façade is its elegant bay window. The dome and domed tower that crown the building originally housed a meteorological and astronomical observatory. The second site is the **FARMÀCIA NADAL** (NADAL PHARMACY. Rambla, 121), a chemist's shop dating from 1850 when it was opened as Farmàcia Masó, which was later transformed into a charming shop featuring multi-coloured mosaics and four red advertising lamps, a good example of Noucentisme (a post-Modernista neoclassical movement).

Casa Elena Castellano

Crossing the Rambla, we find Carrer Canuda and Carrer Santa Anna. A short way into Santa Anna is **CASA ELENA CASTELLANO** (Santa Anna, 21), a 1907 building by Jaume Torres i Grau, a typical Modernista house with its bay windows and floral ornaments. 20

Ateneu Barcelonès - Library

Back to Carrer Canuda, after a few metres you will find the former **PALAU SABASSONA**, of medieval origin. Since 1836 this building is the **ATENEU BARCELONÈS** (Canuda, 6), one of the emblematic cultural entities of the city. Three small jewels remain from Josep Maria Jujol i Gibert and Josep Font i Gumà's 1906 Modernista remodelling : the lift cabin, one of the first to be installed in the city; the reading rooms of the library; and the 21

Romantic-style hanging garden. Continuing down Carrer Canuda you will come to Plaça de la Vila de Madrid, where you can see the remains of a Roman necropolis discovered in 1954 during the redevelopment of the site of the former Discalced Carmelite monastery that had been demolished after the Civil War. The square, redeveloped in 2003, stands on an old Roman access road to the city, and a small section of the original paving can still be seen. The road was flanked by the remains of monolithic funerary monuments and modest tegulae. Carrer Canuda leads into Portal de l'Àngel. A few metres to the left is the building of a gas company, 22 **CATALANA DE GAS, GAS NATURAL** (Portal de l'Àngel, 20-22), a monumental and eclectic building designed by Josep Domènech i Estapà (1895). It was originally built for the Societat Catalana per a l'Enllumenat del Gas, and now contains an interesting Gas Museum exhibiting equipment that shows the evolution of technology for this energy source (tel.: 900 150 366, visits must be booked in advance).

Catalana de Gas - Gas Natural

Going back down Portal de l'Àngel and turning into the small Carrer Montsió, after a few metres you will come to the popular Modernista tavern 23 **ELS QUATRE GATS** (Montsió, 3 bis. For further information see *Let's Go Out*, the guide to Modernista bars and restaurants). This old bar was one of the artistic and cultural centres of the late 19th and early 20th century Barcelona. Ramon Casas, Santiago Rusiñol and Pablo Picasso are some of the illustrious characters who dined, drank and held their artistic gatherings in this unusual bar, which opened in 1897 on the ground floor of the Neo-Gothic **CASA MARTÍ** by Josep Puig i Cadafalch (1896). The building, which looks more European than Catalan in style, features large Gothic-style stained glass windows, a curious

Casa Martí

Inside Els Quatre Gats

decoration on the windows and a Flamboyant-style balcony. The exterior also features sculptures by Eusebi Arnau, wrought iron work by Manuel Ballarín and -in the niche on the corner-Llimona's sculpture of Saint Joseph. What you see now is a replica installed by the City Council in 2000: the original was destroyed during the Spanish Civil War. The inside is no less impressive. Ramon Casas paid for the circular chandeliers and the medieval furniture designed by Puig i Cadafalch. Another of his "gifts" was the painting depicting two men, Pere Romeu, the owner of the bar, and the artist himself riding a tandem; the one currently on display in the establishment is a copy, the original is in the MNAC museum (number **(34)** of the Route). The establishment, which even published its own magazine named *Pèl i Ploma* (*Hair and Quill*), became the haven of artists and intellectuals such as the composers Enric Granados and Isaac Albéniz, and the young painters Joaquim Mir and Pablo Picasso. Unfortunately, the building has not been fully preserved. The original lintel of the door, by Puig i Cadafalch, disappeared in one of the many changes that the premises have undergone in its more than a hundred years of history.

Continuing along Montsió, turn into Carrer de n'Amargós until Carrer Comtal, which takes you to Via Laietana, a wide avenue designed in the second half of the nineteenth century to open a direct access to the old port in an imitation of the North American business centres of the time. The development of this road took several decades, and masters of Modernisme like Domènech i Montaner and especially Puig i Cadafalch contributed to the project.

A short walk up Via Laietana takes us to the **GREMI DELS VELERS** (SAILMAKER'S GUILD, Via Laietana, 50), which is the local association of silk producers since 1764. This magnificent baroque building is decorated by sgraffito representing Atlantes and Cariatids. Slightly hidden behind it one of the essential jewels of Modernisme in Barcelona: the **PALAU DE LA MÚSICA CATALANA** (PALACE OF CATALAN MUSIC). The Palau de la Música was commissioned by the Orfeó Català choral music organisation to the architect Lluís Domènech i Montaner in 1904. The first stone of the new building was laid on Saint George's day 1905 and the 24 ☆

Palau de la Música Catalana
Concert hall

Palau de la Música Catalana

Address	Sant Francesc de Paula, 2.
Open	Guided visits only. Daily 10am to 3.30pm (Summertime, 10am to 6pm)
Information	Tel.: 902 442 882. www.palaumusica.org
Further details	Visits last approxiamtely 50 minutes. Tiquets sold at the shop Les Muses del Palau and at the concert hall ticket booth. Largest group 55 members. Visits in English at every hour o'clock. Timetables may change or be altered by concert hall needs. Updates and information on Route discount at **www.rutadelmodernisme.com** or call 902 076 621.

construction went on for three years. The result was a lavish concert hall for performances of Catalan choral music. The building was located on the site of the former monastery of Sant Francesc de Paula: the small site and the high price of the adjoining land at the time forced Domènech i Montaner to fit the auditorium into a tight grid of streets that limited the views from the exterior, and to find ingenious solutions to provide sufficient space for the stage and to include the offices and archives of the Orfeó in the building.

The church of the former monastery, converted into a parish church, survived until very recently, when it was demolished to provide more space for an extension of the Palau. This project, signed by Oscar Tusquets (2003), used the space to open a square which discovers the huge stained glass windows by Domènech, previously hidden behind the old church. This has been flanked by two cylindrical brick towers, in imitation of Domènech i Montaner, the one on the corner sculpted with the image of a luxuriant

Palau de la Música Catalana
Millet hall, and detail of column

tree. Under the large square is the Petit Palau, a new multi-purpose hall with a capacity for 600 people.

Like La Pedrera, it is a supreme example of Catalan Modernisme, with its bold, brilliant and lavishly decorated architecture. The Palau is one of the most outstanding buildings in the city, and proudly bears the category of UNESCO World Heritage listing. But this was not always the case. The Palau was one of the last extravagances of Modernisme, and even in the 1920s it began to be questioned to such an extent that in the neighbourhood it was known as the "ironmonger's palace", and the architects of the time were in favour of demolishing it. Fortunately, they never achieved their aim and the Palau has become an institution with a special place in the collective memory of Barcelonans.

Palau de la Música Catalana - M. Blay's sculptures

The Palau de la Música Catalana was opened in 1908 with a brief concert of works by Clavé and Händel. The façade of the Palau de la Música struck Barcelonans: of exposed brickwork combined with colourful ceramic mosaics, the corner features sculptures by Miquel Blay in the form of an enormous stone prow, representing an allegory of popular music with two boys and two old men embracing a nymph while Saint George protects them with the Catalan flag flapping in the wind, as it were. This is one of the most characteristic elements of the Palau, a work of great conceptual symbolism. The façade also has a mosaic representing "La balanguera", a poem by Joan Alcover -today the anthem of Majorca island- surrounded by the singers of the Orfeó Català. Other points of interest on the exterior of the Palau are the peculiar ticket offices located inside the columns flanking the main door, now out of use. The rich details continue in the interior: a lavishly decorated foyer, with vaults lined with Valencian tiles and a double stair with golden glass balusters, are the hors d'oeuvres for the true jewel of the building.

The visually overwhelming concert hall is an inebriating succession of sculptures, stained glass, mosaics and decorative elements that constantly play with the perception of light and colour. The most characteristic image of the hall is its enormous and

Palau de la Música Catalana

spectacular skylight of stained glass, which weighs a metric ton. This marvel of lavish art, in the form of an inverted bell, represents a circle of female angels forming a choir around the sun. Domènech i Montaner's obsession with light is not limited to the skylight. He designed the concert hall, with its light steel structure, as a kind of glass box that filters the exterior light through windows that recall those of Gothic cathedrals and help to give the auditorium a sacred atmosphere. The stage of the concert hall is without doubt the most spectacular sculpture in the Palau. The proscenium features an unusual composition in pumice stone designed by Domènech i Montaner and sculpted by Dídac Massana and Pau Gargallo. On the left, the composition includes a bust of Josep Anselm Clavé and an allegory of the flowers of May, representing popular music. On the right, the bust of Beethoven personifies universal music. Above him, Wagnerian valkyries ride silently toward Clavé, symbolising the link between new music and the old Catalan musical folk culture. The stage is completed with a spectacular organ built in Germany and recently restored thanks to popular subscription. The hemicycle designed by Eusebi Arnau and faced with the ceramic fragment *trencadís*, features 18 sculptures that represent the spirits of music, together with a somewhat surprising Austrian coat of arms. A row of balconies and a colonnade of Egyptian influence make a modest contribution to the embellishment of a concert hall that is considered a sanctuary of music, in which musicians of the category of Rubinstein, Menuhin and Pau Casals have performed. Other elements of interest in the hall are the floral motifs that decorate all the ornamental elements, both on the ceiling and on the stained glass, and the mediaeval-like lamps, rather more suited to a castle than to a concert hall. Other spaces of interest in the Palau are the chamber music hall, in which one can still see the founding stone of the building, and the Lluís Millet Hall, which is perhaps the space that remains most faithful to the original design by Domènech i Montaner.

If you go round the Palau along Carrer Amadeu Vives and Carrer Ortigosa you will return to Via Laietana. In front of you stands the triangular building **CAIXA DE PENSIONS I D'ESTALVIS DE BARCELONA** (Via Laietana, 56-58), which for several years housed the Foundation of "la Caixa" savings bank and currently houses the

Administrative Law Section of the High Court of Justice of Catalonia. This Neo-Medieval work (by Enric Sagnier, 1917) bears on its façade a sculpture by Manuel Fuxà conceived as an allegory of thrift, and a spectacular Gothic arch with stained glass windows. On the right is another building, also designed by Sagnier, known as **EDIFICI ANNEX DE LA CAIXA DE PENSIONS** (ANNEXE TO THE CAIXA DE PENSIONS, Jonqueres, 2). Here the architect used predominantly white stone decorated with a few Valencian tiles, but it has more modern lines and is one of the first examples of contemporary office buildings in the city.

At Via Laietana, turn right towards Plaça d'Urquinaona. From this square, the route continues to the left towards Plaça de Catalunya, the nerve centre of the city. Work started on the definitive design of this monumental circular square in 1925, after half a century of litigation between the City Council, the State and the private owners of these lands that for years marked the boundary between the old walled city and the new city that was spreading over the plain. The project was signed by Francesc de Paula Nebot, though he merely adapted an earlier design by Puig i Cadafalch, whom the military regime of general Primo de Rivera had condemned to ostracism. In fact, a work by Josep Puig i Cadafalch in the Modern Classicist style can be seen in the square on the corner of Rambla de Catalunya, **CASA PICH I PON** (PICH I PON HOUSE, Plaça de Catalunya, 9). Plaça de Catalunya marks the start of Passeig de Gràcia and the Eixample district, the true "motherland" of Barcelona's Modernisme. In the middle of the square is the underground Tourist Information Office of Barcelona, the starting point for the Modernisme Walking Tours and one of the three Modernisme Centres of Barcelona. You can obtain the free discount vouchers for the Modernisme Route on presenting this guide at the Centre, which specialises in information on Modernisme. The adjacent shop sells products related to this artistic movement.

Centre d'Informació de Turisme de Barcelona - Centre del Modernisme

Address	Plaça de Catalunya, 17, basement.
Open	**Modernisme Centre:** Monday to Saturday from 10am to 7pm and Sundays and public holidays from 10am to 2pm Closed on 1 and 6 January and 25 and 26 December. **Modernisme Walking Tours:** Saturdays and Sundays at 4pm Languages: Catalan, Spanish and English. On January 1st and 6 and December 25 and 26 there are no Walking Tours. Tourist Information Office: Monday to Sunday from 9am to 9pm Closed on January 1st and December 25. Open on December 26 from 9am to 3pm and on January 6 from 3 to 9pm
Information	**Modernisme Centre:** Tel.: 902 076 621. www.rutadelmodernisme.com **Tourist Information Centre:** Tel.: 932 853 832. www.barcelonaturisme.com
Further details	Opening times and languages may vary; you are advised to check beforehand. Consult the Route discount for Walking Tours on the website **www.rutadelmodernisme.com** or phone: 902 076 621.

L'Eixample

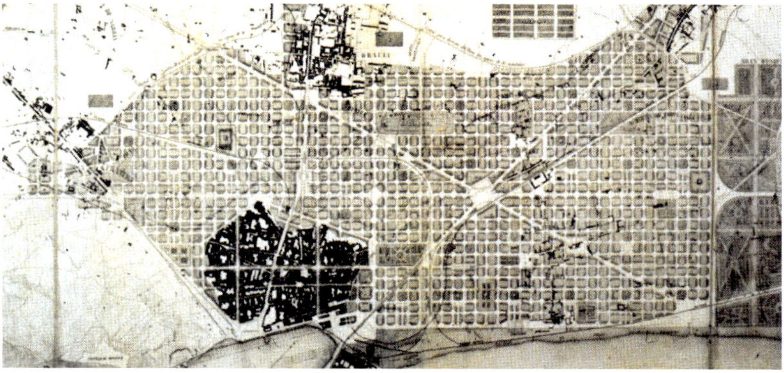

Cerda's project for l'Eixample

The expansion area called "l'Eixample" was first conceived in the mid-19th century. In 1854, the city obtained the necessary authorisation from the government to knock down the walls that surrounded Barcelona. The walls, which were not popular since 1714, as they had been used to control the city rather than to defend it, rose on the line now followed by Av. del Paral·lel and the "Rondes" Sant Pau, Sant Antoni, Universitat, Sant Pere, and Passeig de Lluís Companys. However, despite enthusiastic volunteers who started knocking down parts on their own, the city walls were not removed completely until some years later. The demolition took almost a decade and was thorough. In 1859, with the city walls half demolished, development work began on the zone between the original town centre of Barcelona and the plain on which the old towns of Gràcia, Sants, Les Corts, Sant Gervasi de Cassoles and Sant Martí de Provençals were located. This initial zone of the Eixample occupied the former military security zone of two kilometres - the range of cannonballs- surrounding the city walls.

The Eixample is characterised by its grid plan, designed in 1859 by the engineer and town planner Ildefons Cerdà. Cerdà's design is somewhat reminiscent of the Paris that Haussman designed for Napoleon 3rd, with its wide boulevards running right through the centre of the city. The main difference was that Cerdà did not have an urban centre to work on. He was faced with a large expanse of open country -a delight for any planner. A man of socialist leanings, Cerdà devised an urban grid plan in which each block represented society and allowed for the cohabitation of the bourgeoisie, craftsmen, tradesmen and workers in a city without hierarchies. But Cerdà's ideal was never realised. The dynamics of real estate soon led some areas of the Eixample to become more expensive and exclusive than others. The border between two zones was marked by the railway line built in 1863 to link Plaça de Catalunya to the town of Sarrià along the present-day Carrer Balmes (the railway was placed underground in 1929 and is now the FGC 6 and 7 subway lines). On the left of the lines the land was cheaper; on the right it was far more expensive. This is why the Modernista architecture built to satisfy the vanity of the flourishing bourgeoisie of the time is mostly concentrated to the right of Carrer Balmes.

This is not the only divergence between Cerdà's utopian design and reality in the Eixample. Cerdà designed 550 open gardened blocks separated by 20-metre wide streets. The purpose of the 45 degree-chamfered corners was to provide sufficient turning space for public transport vehicles and to create a place for loading and unloading of goods. Except for this last one, none of the original plans of Cerdà have been fulfilled. The current blocks are closed and the interior garden courts have been replaced almost completely by warehouses or garages. The 17-metre height planned by Cerdà was not respected, nor were his prescriptions of a 4,000 m^2 maximum housing density per block, which developers promptly raised to 16,000 m^2.

The construction of the new district designed by Cerdà, which started in 1860, was slow and discontinuous. The first buildings of the Eixample were those that occupied the corners on the crossing of Carrer Roger de Llúria with Carrer Consell de Cent (they are now identified by a plate on the façade). In 1872, there were only one thousand houses concentrated almost exclusively in the area between Passeig de Gràcia and the streets Consell de Cent, Casp and Bailèn -one thousand buildings for the first 40,000 inhabitants of a district that did not start to grow steadily until 1880, when a new generation of architects who were more ambitious and talented than their predecessors led the construction of the new Barcelona. These architects (with Gaudí, Puig i Cadafalch and Domènech i Montaner at the head) transformed the Eixample into an open-air museum of dwellings with a good layout, ventilation and lighting -functional dwellings, as we would call them today. These houses were thus the most modern at the beginning of the 20th century. Despite all the distortions of Cerdà's original design, the Eixample is one of the most interesting urban areas in Europe. During the last few years, the City Council has promoted the recovery of some block interiors to open them to the public.

Passeig de Gràcia is the backbone of the Eixample. It is a boulevard with a mixture of private residences, banks, cinemas, prestige establishments, coffee bars and many treasures of Modernisme. Initially, the boulevard was a simple dirt track that ran from the city walls of Barcelona to the neighbouring town of Gràcia. This began to change in 1827, when it was converted into a tree-lined boulevard. In 1852, the first gaslights were installed, and one year later a large leisure zone called Camps Elisis with gardens, bars, restaurants, dance halls, amusements and an open-air auditorium, was opened in the section between Carrer Aragó and Carrer Mallorca. In 1872 the first horse-drawn tramway began to operate, and from the 1890's onward it became the new residential centre of the upper middle classes. The fact that it is a wealthy area is shown in one of the most striking elements of the Passeig: its 31 benches-cum-streetlamps, designed in 1906 by Pere Falqués **(55)**, which may pass unnoticed among the diversity of modern urban elements and the swarming traffic that invades Passeig de Gràcia every day. Other characteristic elements are the panots (pavement tiles), copied from the floor tiles designed by Gaudí for Casa Batlló, which were finally installed in the kitchens and service areas of La Pedrera. In 2002 the City Council repaved the avenue with them: hexagonal tiles that are all alike yet when set together reveal the marine motifs: an octopus, a conch and a starfish. The tiles were produced by the company Escofet and were among the first mass-produced paving tiles in Catalonia.

25 The architectural marvels of Passeig de Gràcia begin almost at the bottom of the boulevard with **CASA PASCUAL I PONS** (PASCUAL I PONS HOUSE. Passeig de Gràcia, 2-4), at the closing of this edition, restoration work had begun the most Gothic work by Enric Sagnier i Villavecchia, one of the most prolific Modernista architects of Barcelona. The main interest of the building lies in the interior: it has stained glass windows representing medieval figures that can be seen from the exterior, a staircase with sculptural decorative elements and iron and glass lamps, and

Casa Pascual i Pons

Casa Llorenç Camprubí

a majestic wooden fireplace. Built in 1890-1891, the Casa Pons i Pascual was originally two separate houses designed individually to make full use of their exceptional location, at the corner of Plaça de Catalunya and Passeig de Gràcia. A major remodelling of the houses was undertaken in 1984. The Route now continues up Passeig de Gràcia to Carrer Casp, where it is worth making a brief detour. → page 62

The first noteworthy building that you come to is the Modernista **CASA LLORENÇ CAMPRUBÍ** (LLORENÇ CAMPRUBÍ HOUSE. Casp, 22) by Adolf Ruiz i Casamitjana (1901). 26 With an exceptional bay window that occupies the piano nobile and the first floor of the building, Casa Camprubí is a good example of Ruiz's work in the late nineteenth century, a period in which this architect made a very personal interpretation of a wide repertory of Neo-Gothic forms and elements. The following building on the detour along Carrer Casp is **CASA SALVADÓ** (SALVADÓ HOUSE. Casp, 46), an Eclectic-style alternative by Juli Batllevell in a zone dominated by Modernisme. The adjoining building is **CASA CALVET** (CALVET HOUSE. Casp, 48) by Antoni Gaudí. 27 ☆ Casa Calvet (1898-1899) was the first residential building by the brilliant architect in the Eixample, and with it he started a line that was followed by many houses that also used Baroque or Rococo elements such as the undulating forms, the peculiar treatment of the irregular surface of Montjuïc sandstone, the balconies and the bay windows. In Casa Calvet, Gaudí gave a different treatment to each element of the building. The façade features a Baroque bay window with wrought iron railings and reliefs representing different types of fungi in reference to the fact that Eduard Calvet, the first owner of the building, was an amateur mycologist. The decoration of the bay window includes the coat of arms of Catalonia and a representation of a cypress tree, symbol of hospitality. This is shown in the foyer and the ground floor premises, which have now been transformed into the **Casa Calvet Restaurant** (tables must be booked in advance: phone 934 124 012. For further information see *Let's Go Out*, the guide to Modernista bars and restaurants). The restaurant has conserved the original furniture of Calvet's office, from which he ran his textile emporium. Interesting features are the lamps, the benches in the reception room and the courtesy benches against the wall, the wood partitions that separated the offices from the textile store, the door handles and the beams of the ceiling.

Casa Calvet

28 If you now retrace your steps along Carrer Casp to Passeig de Gràcia, you will come to the **CASES ROCAMORA** buildings (ROCAMORA HOUSES. Passeig de Gràcia, 6-14). Like the Casa de les Punxes by Puig i Cadafalch **(78)**, this is one of the largest architectural complexes in the Eixample. Though the blocks of this district were normally divided into individual buildings, this site was built as a single architectural volume to emphasise its magnificence. It is a 1914 building in a clearly Neo-Gothic style by the brothers Joaquim and Bonaventura Bassegoda, who paid special attention to the treatment of the stone on the façade and to the striking set of bay windows on the corner of Carrer Casp.

Cases Rocamora

The route continues up Passeig de Gràcia to Gran Via de les Corts Catalanes, one of the three road arteries that Cerdà designed to communicate the whole grid plan of the Eixample (the other two are Avinguda Diagonal and Avinguda Meridiana). The crossing of these two large avenues is dominated by two striking buildings, though not Modernista in style. On the left is **PALAU MARCET** (MARCET PALACE. Passeig de Gràcia, 13), an urban mansion built in 1887 by Tiberi Sabater, which was transformed in 1934 into a theatre and has now been converted into a multi-screen cinema. On the right is the undulating Rationalist façade decorated with glass bricks of **JOIERIA ROCA** (Passeig de Gràcia, 18), a jeweller's shop designed by Josep Lluís Sert in 1934. → page 70

A detour to the left along Gran Via de les Corts Catalanes leads to several interesting Modernista buildings, but the first building is the Eclectic style **CASA PIA BATLLÓ** (PIA BATLLÓ HOUSE. Rambla de Catalunya, 17), a Neo-Gothic building by Josep Vilaseca (1896) that stands on the corner and is topped by two glazed ceramic towers crowned by wrought iron belvederes. After passing the monumental Cine Coliseum and the Neo-Classical building of the University of Barcelona (by Elies Rogent, 1896), on the opposite side of the avenue -on what Barcelonans call "the seaward
29 side" of any street- you can see the **CASA GERÓNIMO GRANELL** (GERÓNIMO GRANELL HOUSE. Gran Via de les Corts Catalanes, 582) by the architect Gerónimo F. Granell i Barrera (1902). Though this building has undergone many transformations on the ground floor, it still has Modernista elements such as the bay window next to the party wall, whose location breaks the symmetry of the façade. A full restoration in 2004 has recovered some of the original flavour of this architect's peculiar use of Neo-Gothic forms.

Casa Gerónimo Granell

Farmàcia Mestre

Further along, at the corner of Carrer Villarroel, you will come to a set of three Modernista
30 buildings by unknown architects, **CONJUNT DE TRES EDIFICIS** (ENSEMBLE OF THREE BUILDINGS. Gran Via de les Corts Catalanes, 536-542 / Villarroel, 49-51), where the **FARMÀCIA MESTRE** (MESTRE PHARMACY) (1903), a chemist's shop located on the ground floor at the corner of Gran Via and Carrer Villarroel, still has much of its original decoration, especially the doors and shop windows. Continuing along Gran Via, at the corner of Carrer Comte Borrell, it is worth spending a few moments at another chemist's shop which shows Modernista influences, the **FARMÀCIA MADROÑAL** (MADROÑAL PHARMACY. Comte Borrell, 133).

Farmàcia Madroñal

Casa Golferichs

Very close by, on the opposite side - Barcelonans would call this "the mountain side" of the road- you will come to the **CASA GOLFERICHS** (GOLFERICHS HOUSE. Gran Via de les Corts Catalanes, 491), a Modernista house built in 1901 by Joan Rubió i Bellvé for Macari Golferichs, a tropical wood trader. After the Civil War it became a religious school and in the late 1960s it was bought by a private developer with the idea of demolishing it and building flats. But the insistent protests of the neighbours prevented "el Xalet", as it is popularly known, from falling victim to speculation. In 1980 the Barcelona City Council recovered the ownership of the building to convert it into a civic centre. In 2004 it was opened after a restoration that included the façades, the roofs, the stone walls, the woodwork and the ceramics. 31

Casa de la Lactància

Next you will come to **CASA DE LA LACTÀNCIA** (NURSING MOTHER'S HOUSE. Gran Via de les Corts Catalanes, 475-477), a beautiful blue building with a sculptural relief that indicates the original use of the building. One of the main points of interest of the house, completed in 1913 by Antoni de Falguera i Sivilla and Pere Falqués i Urpí, is the entrance court decorated with ceramics and crowned by a skylight that fills it with light. Just before reaching Plaça d'Espanya, you will pass in front of **CASA FAJOL** (FAJOL HOUSE. Llançà, 20), by Josep Graner i Prat (1912), popularly known as the "Butterfly House" because of the *trencadís* crown representing a butterfly with unusual curved lines that is the identifying feature of the building. 32

Casa Fajol

33

Gran Via de les Corts Catalanes will take you to Plaça d'Espanya, a traffic hub of the city, where you enter the Sants district, an area with a traditional atmosphere that still shows its industrial and working class history. This may be why there are few traces of Modernisme here, except for a few emblematic buildings. In the middle of the square is the **FONT COMMEMORATIVA DE L'EXPOSICIÓ DE 1929** (COMMEMORATIVE FOUNTAIN OF THE 1929 EXHIBITION. Plaça d'Espanya, s/n), built by Josep M. Jujol for the entrance square to the International Exhibition of Barcelona of 1929, though it was not finished until after the exhibition. It has groups of sculptures by Miquel Blay and by the brothers Miquel and Llucià Oslé, and is considered to be Eclectic in style.

Go up Avinguda de la Reina Maria Cristina to the Palau Nacional; if this avenue is closed to the public because of a trade fair of Fira de Barcelona (see www.rutadelmodernisme.com or phone 902 076 621), go up Carrer Mèxic. Continue walking up the **ESCALES I MIRADOR DEL PALAU NACIONAL** (STEPS AND VIEWPOINT OF THE NATIONAL PALACE), the backbone of the 1929 Exhibition, designed by the architect Josep Puig i Cadafalch, which contains three squares on different levels with waterfalls in the centre, all arranged with precise symmetry. In the first square is the **FONT MÀGICA** (MAGIC FOUNTAIN. Plaça de Carles Buïgas, s/n), built by the engineer Carles Buïgas in 1927-29, which takes its name from the impression it caused among the public of the time. One can regularly see the spectacle of water, music, light and colour (information calling 010). Continuing up the steps, you will come to Plaça del Marquès de Foronda. It is flanked on either side by the **PALAU D'ALFONS XIII** (ALFONS XIII PALACE) and the **PALAU DE LA REINA VICTÒRIA EUGÈNIA** (QUEEN VICTÒRIA EUGÈNIA PALACE), which were designed in 1918-1923 by Josep Puig i Cadafalch as pavilions for the 1929 Exhibition and are now used for the trade fairs of Fira de Barcelona.

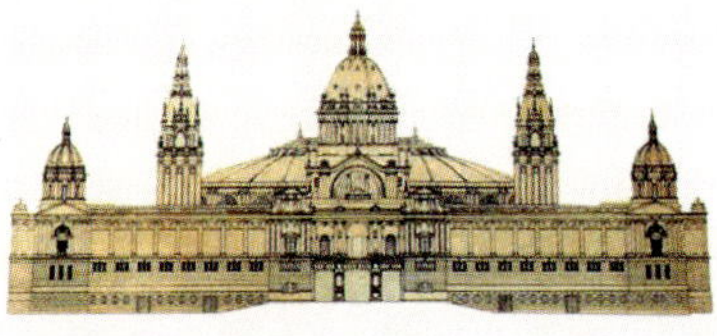
Palau Nacional - MNAC

The rise ends right in front of the majestic **PALAU NACIONAL** (NATIONAL PALACE), which

MNAC - Museu Nacional d'Art de Catalunya

Address	Palau Nacional, Parc de Montjuïc, 08038 Barcelona.
Open	Tuesday to Saturday, 10am to 7pm. Sundays and holidays, 10am to 2.30pm. Closed on Mondays (except holidays) and on January 1st, May 1st and December 25th.
Information	Tel.: 902 076 621. info@mnac.es; www.mnac.es
Further details	Tiquet booths close at 6.30pm; 2pm on Sundays and holidays. Timetables may vary. Updates and information on Route discount at **www.rutadelmodernisme.com** or call 902 076 621.

was the main hall of the International Exhibition. Built between 1927 and 1929 to the design by Eugeni P. Cendoya and Enric Catà, with the collaboration of Pere Domènech i Roura, this edifice falls within the style known as Eclectic Monumentalism. It currently houses the **MNAC, MUSEU NACIONAL D'ART DE CATALUNYA** (NATIONAL ART MUSEUM OF CATALONIA.), 34 ☆ which since 2004, on completion of the rehabilitation work on the building, has finally regrouped all its collections. These collections embrace over a thousand years of Catalan art: painting, sculpture, arts of the object, drawing and engraving, photography, numismatics and medals. Naturally, this includes a good exhibition of Catalan art from the mid-19th to

MNAC - Gaudí, 1907: double seat for Casa Batlló

MNAC - Ramon Casas, 1893 - *Study*

the mid-20th century. The collection of the MNAC is the most representative of the Modernista movement in Barcelona, displaying the most salient works of this artistic style in all their diversity: painting, sculpture and decorative arts.

A visit to the Museum is also essential in order to place the work of the Modernista architects in the artistic context of their time. For example, though Gaudí did not frequent the Modernista coteries, he was friendly -and there were mutual artistic influences- with several artists who belonged to the movement, such as the sculptors Josep Llimona and Carles Mani and the painters Joaquim Mir, Anglada i Camarasa, Francesc Gimeno and Darío de Regoyos, all of whom are represented in the collections of the Museum. Many of the works on display refer to sites on the Barcelona Modernisme Route. Here one can see, for example, the original work *Ramon Casas and Pere Romeu on a tandem* (1897) by the painter Ramon Casas (1866-1932), which decorated Els Quatre Gats **(23)**, where you have seen a copy. The rich collection of decorative arts of the Museum shows us the interior decor of the main floors of some of the most emblematic houses of Modernista architecture, such as those that form the famous "Mansana de la Discòrdia" on Passeig de Gràcia. The Museum shows several elements of the furniture from Casa Amatller **(44)**, by the architect Josep Puig i Cadafalch, such as a bench, a glass cabinet and a ceiling light designed by the architect himself. It exhibits several designs by Antoni Gaudí from Casa Batlló **(45)**, such as a sliding door, a chair and a sofa that is very characteristic of his style. The architect Lluís Domènech i Montaner, who designed the Casa Lleó Morera **(43)**, commissioned the interior decoration of the main floor of the building to the Majorcan cabinetmaker Gaspar Homar (1870-1953), one of the main figures of Modernista decorative arts. His designs won prizes in Barcelona, Madrid, London (1907) and Paris (1909). Of this decoration, the Museum exhibits almost the complete living room, as well as other elements from the rest of the dwelling, such as a sofa with glass cabinets and inlaid panelling at the sides. To complete the vision of modern art in Catalonia, visitors should not neglect the work of other artists and movements from before -Marià Fortuny and the followers of the Rome School- and after Modernisme. The second generation of Modernista artists such as Joaquim Mir; the artists of the Noucentista period such as Joaquim Sunyer, Joaquim Torres Garcia and Manolo Hugué; and the avant-garde sculptures of Gargallo and Juli González are especially interesting.

From MNAC, go down to Plaça de Carles Buïgas and take Avinguda del Marquès de Comillas to the

☆ 35 **CAIXAFORUM - ANTIGA FÀBRICA CASARAMONA** (FORMER CASARAMONA FACTORY. Av. Marquès de Comillas, 6-8). The entrepreneur Casimir Casaramona decided to locate his textile factory on Montjuïc hill and contracted Josep Puig i Cadafalch to design it in 1912. The result was a typical complex of industrial architecture including Catalan vaults, ceramics and artificial stone. Puig i Cadafalch also gave the

The old Casaramona factory, now CaixaForum

Antiga Fàbrica Casaramona - CaixaForum

Address	Marquès de Comillas, 6
Open	Tuesday to Sunday and on public holidays, 10am to 8pm.
Information	Tel.: 934 768 600. info.fundacio@lacaixa.es www.fundacio.lacaixa.es
Further details	Free entrance. Check updates and information on Route discount at **www.rutadelmodernisme.com** or call 902 076 621

complex his characteristic Neo-Gothic style and highly personal details such as the pinnacles and the square towers. The factory, the largest building designed by Puig i Cadafalch, eventually fell into disuse and from 1940 it housed the stables of the National Police cavalry. Fortunately, in 1998 it was rehabilitated to house CaixaForum, the new headquarters and cultural centre of "la Caixa" savings bank's Foundation. Exhibitions, workshops, lectures, courses and concerts are a few of the activities offered by CaixaForum, which organises guided visits to the exhibitions and to the Modernista building.

Magòria Station

Hostafrancs Market

Continuing along Gran Via towards Hospitalet de Llobregat, you will come to the **ESTACIÓ DE LA MAGÒRIA** (MAGÒRIA STATION. Gran Via de les Corts Catalanes, 181-247 / Moianès, 1-17), built by Josep Domènech i Estapà in 1912 for the goods trains travelling to the port and linking with the FGC railway line that runs under Gran Via. The station and the adjoining land have been converted into a sports complex. Not far away, at the end of Carrer Moianès, we come to Carrer de la Creu Coberta, where you may see two fine examples of early Modernisme. On the right you will find the **MERCAT D'HOSTAFRANCS** (HOSTAFRANCS MARKET. Creu Coberta, 93), built in 1888 by Antoni Rovira i Trías and featuring an attractive iron structure like that of the Sant Antoni Market by the same engineer. Across

36

37

the street, the Former Deputy Mayor's Office

38 of Hostafrancs, currently the **SEU DEL DISTRICTE DE SANTS-MONTJUÏC** (SANTS-MONTJUÏC DISTRICT HALL. Creu Coberta, 106), completed in two stages by Jaume Gustà i Bondia (1895) and Ubald Iranzo i Eiras (1908-1915). Partially Modernista and partially eclectic in style, the main features of this town hall are the stained glass windows by Francesc Labarta.

Seu del Districte de Sants - Montjuïc

39 Back on Passeig de Gràcia, a little further up, on the left side is the **CASA MALAGRIDA** (MALAGRIDA HOUSE. Passeig de Gràcia, 27) built in 1908 by Joaquim Codina i Matalí. Like other buildings of the time located in the best area of the Eixample, Casa Malagrida has the exterior appearance of an urban mansion that avoids the usual style of residential buildings in the Eixample. Nevertheless, it was originally designed as a dwelling for several families. The most outstanding features of the building are the spectacular dome and the wrought iron lamp-posts in a foyer in which the elegant frescos and the coffered ceiling are also worth seeing.

→ page 72

Continue up Passeig de Gràcia and turn right at Carrer Consell de Cent, following the direction of the traffic. After walking two blocks you will come to the origin of the Eixample itself: the first houses that were built in the district. The **CASES CERDÀ** (CERDÀ HOUSES) were built in 1864 by Antoni Valls on the corners of Carrer Consell de Cent and Carrer Roger de Llúria. They have been restored and are identified by a plate on the façade.

Some distance on, we will see the **CONFITERIA J. REÑÉ** (J. REÑÉ'S CONFECTIONERY, Consell de Cent, 362), an old Modernista bakers' which is currently a cafe-restaurant.

Casa Malagrida

A little further along, at Carrer Girona, there is an 1898 Modernista bakery, **FORN SARRET** (SARRET BAKERY. Girona, 73), with delightful marquetry doors and a coat of arms above the door depicting an allegory of the wheat harvest. On the opposite corner is the 1900 bakery **FORN DE LA CONCEPCIÓ** (Girona, 74), by Josep Suñer. 40 41

Forn Sarret

Forn de la Concepció

Casa Pomar

Going a little further up Carrer Girona, you will come to **CASA POMAR** (POMAR HOUSE. Girona, 86), an original 1904-1906 design by Rubió i Bellvé, with a façade that gives it the appearance of a church (don't miss the green ceramics in the shape of a ship's keel over the main door). Going back along Carrer Consell de Cent, not far away on Carrer Roger de Llúria between Carrer Consell de Cent and Carrer Diputació is the **TORRE DE LES AIGÜES** (WATER TOWER. Roger de Llúria, 56), built in 1867 by Josep Oriol Mestres. In 1987 it became the first inner court to be recovered by the City Council according to Cerdà's initial design. In summer this place becomes an urban beach for the neighbours. Opposite is Passatge Permanyer, a charming lane of small houses that recalls Victorian London. 42

The Route now returns to Passeig de Gràcia. The following stage on the tour of the Modernista buildings of Barcelona is the **MANSANA DE LA DISCÒRDIA** (Block of Discord), the 100 metres of Barcelona street that contain three masterpieces by the three main Modernista arquitects: Lluís Domènech i Montaner (Casa Lleó Morera), Josep Puig i Cadafalch (Casa Amatller) and Antoni Gaudí (Casa Batlló). The block was given this name because of the presumed visual incompatibility of the three large buildings that share this section of Passeig de Gràcia between Carrer Consell de Cent and Carrer Aragó, which-curiously enough-are conversions of previously existing buildings.

43 The first building of interest in this unique Mansana de la Discòrdia is the **CASA LLEÓ MORERA** (LLEÓ MORERA HOUSE. Passeig de Gràcia, 35), which unfortunately cannot be visited inside. In 1905, Lluís Domènech i Montaner converted this house built in 1864 by the Sociedad Fomento del Ensanche in order to improve it and redecorate it for its new owners, the Lleo Morera family. The most Renaissance-influenced architect of Modernisme in Barcelona combined in Casa Lleó Morera -a small and even modest work- the creative effort of a considerable number of artists and craftsmen who worked in close collaboration to achieve a surprising, almost miraculous result in the purest Domènech i Montaner floral style. From the foyer to the staircase, the lift and the piano nobile, the Casa Lleó

Casa Lleó Morera

Casa Lleó Morera - Mosaic by Lluís Bru

Morera is one of the richest and best preserved examples of applied arts in the Modernista style, featuring mosaics, stained glass, marquetry, paving and sculptures. The main feature of the house is precisely one of the great surprises of Modernisme in Barcelona: a monumental stained glass window by Antoni Rigalt that occupies the former main dining room of the house and represents a bucolic rural scene (see photo on page 25). The same room has eight panels of ceramic work with porcelain figures in relief and lintels in which Eusebi Arnau sculpted a Provençal legend, *La dida de l'Infant Rei (The Child King's Nanny)*. On the façade his sculptural work was also spectacular, but the

Sofa designed by Gaspar Homar for Casa Lleó Morera, now in the MNAC

Josep Puig i Cadafalch (1867-1956)

Josep Puig i Cadafalch was born in 1867 in a well-to-do family of Mataró, a thriving industrial city north of Barcelona. He soon stood out for his intelligence and precocity: at the age of sixteen he was already giving lectures and publishing articles, particularly on Romanesque art, the great passion of his life. He was eventually to be considered a world authority on the subject, to which he contributed his massive trilogy *L'arquitectura romànica de Catalunya* (1909-1918), and was awarded five honorary doctorates in Europe and the United States.

At the age of 25, shortly after graduation at the School of Architecture of Barcelona (one of his professors was Domènech i Montaner), Puig was already the municipal architect of Mataró, where he built a new market (1892) and designed a modern sewage system (1895). Meanwhile, he undertook private commissions, some of them major mansions such as the Casa Coll i Regàs in Mataró and the Casa Garí "el Cros" in Argentona, both in 1898. He was soon in demand in Barcelona, where in 1895 he began to work on the Casa Martí, and proceeded to plan Casa Amatller and Casa Macaya. Also in this period he began to promote and participate in a series of archaeological projects (like the Greek-Roman site of Empúries, the Romanesque remains of Sant Pere de Rodes, or the Visigothic churches of Sant Pere in Terrassa) and museum projects (in particular the collection of Romanesque painting of the present-day MNAC), which are today fundamental works of the art history of Catalonia.

The early involvement of Puig with the city of Barcelona led him to become a city councillor in 1901. This marked the start of a long political career, during which he was member of the Spanish Congress and for many years deputy of the provincial council. In 1917 he succeeded Prat de la Riba as president of the Mancomunitat ("Commonwealth") of Catalonia, a first attempt at autonomous regional government that had been set up three years earlier. As could not be otherwise, Puig i Cadafalch was a prolific and versatile president, despite the lack of real power and the shortage of resources. Thus, as a good Modernista, he worked to develop the country by providing it with the infrastructures proper to a modern state, through projects involving the creation of public technical and professional schools such as the School of Nursing, the School of Commerce and the School of Textile Industries; the systematic extension of the telephone network to the country; the promotion of social welfare organisations such as the first organisation of the blind and the Maternity Hospital; and the foundation of Catalan scientific institutions such as the IEC (the Catalan scientific academy), the future MNAC and the Library of Catalonia. Occupying the Presidency, however, did not prevent him from continuing with his work as an architect and town planner: the fact that the president was commissioned to direct public municipal works such as the development of Via Laietana and the planning of the enclosure for the International Exhibition of 1929, clearly illustrates what the Catalan bourgeois of the period were able to do for themselves.

The coup d'état by General Primo de Rivera in 1923, which the conservative Puig met with reserved optimism, led a year later to the abolition of the Mancomunitat and the prohibition of all Catalan political and cultural activities. In addition to losing his post, Puig i Cadafalch was condemned to a professional and public ostracism that, one way or another, was to accompany him for the rest of his life. In 1936, at the outbreak of the Civil War, the Puig family went into exile in France and did not return until 1942. In the new Spanish fascist regime, the old Catalan nationalist still carried out a few architectural projects, though they often had to be signed by other architects in order to receive approval. He died in Barcelona in 1956.

female figures on the arches of the ground floor were mutilated in the 1940s when the sculptures and the remaining ornamental details were destroyed to allow new shop windows to be fitted. This was partially restored in 1992 thanks to photographs and documents. In the MNAC **(34)** you can see elements of interior decor of the main floor such as furniture, lamps and carpets designed by Gaspar Homar. One of the outstanding exhibits is a huge sofa-cupboard of marquetry work.

Adjoining **Casa Lleó Morera** are two buildings that provide a perfect yet discreet counterpoint, contemporary to the large works of the Mansana de la Discòrdia. The first of these is the **CASA MULLERAS** (MULLERAS HOUSE. Passeig de Gràcia, 37), a sober 1911 architectural work by Enric Sagnier that was also the conversion of a previous building, dating from 1868, which included the complete replacement of the façade. The second is **CASA BONET** (BONET HOUSE. Passeig de Gràcia, 39), a rather undistinguished Classicist work by Jaume Brossa (1901), which nevertheless houses a delightful little Perfume Museum on the ground floor. Opened in 1961, it shows a collection of almost 5,000 perfume bottles and phials from different cultures and civilisations, ranging from Egyptian, Greek, Roman, Carthaginian, Arabic and Oriental bottles of pottery and glass to an interesting collection of phials from the 17th to the 19th century in porcelain, crystal glass and other noble materials.

Casa Amatller

The next essential stop on Mansana de la Discòrdia is **CASA AMATLLER** (AMATLLER HOUSE). **44** ☆ The history of this building changed

Casa Amatller

between 1898 and 1900, when the chocolate manufacturer Antoni Amatller, who was also a philanthropist, amateur photographer and glasswork collector, bought an uninteresting building erected in 1875 in Passeig de Gràcia to use as his main residence. The manufacturer commissioned the work to the architect Josep Puig i Cadafalch, who decided to give it the appearance of an urban Gothic mansion, with a flat façade and a central court with a staircase leading to the piano nobile.

Puig i Cadafalch made a highly personal reading of the Neo-Gothic style in the Casa Amatller, through a design that allowed him to maintain the excellence of his work even at a time when the elements of Gothic language had been abandoned by most architects. The first outstanding feature in the building is its stepped Nordic façade, coated by a sgraffito membrane of ochre and white stucco and crowned by an extravagant Flemish-style gable adorned with red and gold vitrified Valencian tiles.

The façade, considered by some specialists to be "the apotheosis of the decorative arts" and in which some have seen influences of the town houses of Copenhagen, Brussels and Amsterdam, has a bay window of Wagnerian inspiration that recalls the façade of the Sant Jordi Chapel in the Palau de la Generalitat (Plaça de Sant Jaume). Puig i Cadafalch sprinkled the house with his typical mediaeval details. The entrance, for example, is decorated with sculptures, capitals and stucco work such as the stone figure of Saint George killing the dragon by Eusebi Arnau. The figures on the windows of the main floor recall the fantastic and grotesque creatures that decorate Gothic mansions and churches. Also on the ground floor there is a jeweller's shop that has respected the small original windows with floral ornamentation that are inspired by Catalan Gothic mansions.

The foyer is decorated with three bronze lamps and has an elegant staircase leading to the piano nobile, which houses the Amatller Institute of Hispanic Art, founded by the Amatller family, an academic institution dedicated to the study of Spanish art that currently owns the

Casa Amatller

building. The main floor is one of the few interiors of Barcelona that still conserve not only much of the original wealth of ornamentation, but also the opulent gilded atmosphere enjoyed by the bourgeoisie of the Modernista Eixample, thanks to the sculptures that adapt to the spaces, the floors of Roman-style mosaic and white marble, and the ceilings that offer a rich combination of polychrome beams and sgraffito work. The fireplace is one of the most outstanding features, though many consider that the masterpiece of this floor is the pink marble column located right in the middle of the bay window, which can be seen from the street -it plays no structural role, but is merely a hedonistic feature, only intended to offer the pure pleasure of contemplation. Unfortunately, this house is not open to visitors, but you can see several pieces of the original furniture at the MNAC **(34)**.

☆ **45** The third great work of the Mansana de la Discòrdia is **CASA BATLLÓ** (BATLLÓ HOUSE.) Josep Batlló was an ostentatious textile tycoon who owned several factories, one of them the old Vapor Batlló on Carrer Urgell, which is now the Industrial School of Barcelona. In 1904 he commissioned Antoni Gaudí to remodel an original building dating from 1870, and his fabulous riches allowed the architect to set his imagination free -indeed, Gaudí reportedly declared his intention to create "a paradise on earth".

Casa Batlló

Address	Passeig de Gràcia, 43.
Open	Daily 9am to 8pm. Closed on January 1st and December 25th.
Information	Tel.: 934 880 666 or 932 160 306. Fax: 934 883 090.
Further details	Audioguides in English and other languages. Adapted to the visually and/or physically impaired. Timetables may change. Check updates and information on Route discount at **www.rutadelmodernisme.com** or call 902 076 621.

He added a fifth floor, built the basement, extended the foyer, rebuilt the staircase and interior walls, and used wide curves in all the rooms. In fact, the building has no right angles. But the most singular element of the house is the façade, which combines

stone on the ground floor and the piano nobile with a mosaic facing on the higher floors, and is crowned with a scaly tiled roof that recalls a reptile's back. The interpretation of the façade has long been a source of dispute. For some, Gaudí's aim was to build a symbolic hymn of the legend of Saint George, the patron saint of Catalonia, in his mythological victory over the dragon. If the roof is the dragon's back and the circular tower symbolises Saint George's lance, the iron balconies of the intermediate floors represent the skulls of the dragon's victims, and the bay window on the first floor simulates the bones and tendons left over after the dragon's feasts. However, another interpretation of Casa Batlló is that the whole façade is an allegory of Carnival. Then the roof would be a harlequin's hat, the balconies would clearly represent ball masks, and the multicolour trencadís ceramic which "cascades" down the façade -the work of a young Josep Maria Jujol- would be the confetti of the feast.

The inside is even more spectacular than the façade. The light well of the Casa Batlló is a true marvel. Always obsessed by lighting, Gaudí gave it an irregular facing of tiles that become darker, going from pearl grey to cobalt blue, as they go up toward the skylight. The result of this almost subliminal architectural device is an equal distribution of natural lighting on all floors. To complete the effect, the balconies and windows of the lower floors are larger than those on the upper floors. The staircase leading to the main floor is wrung like the skeleton of a fossilised dinosaur and the sinuous

walls, painted to resemble a mosaic, have a surface and reflections resembling a cave eroded by the sea. The main floor is exceptionally well-preserved. The counterweights that are used to raise the stained glass windows giving onto Passeig de Gràcia are still fully operative, as are the grilles that provide air from the street -a brilliant natural ventilation system- and the precise hand-made window and door fastenings. On this floor, however, there are only two original pieces of furniture designed by Gaudí, a desk and a bench, but other designs by Gaudí for Casa Batlló may be seen at the MNAC **(34)**.

Casa Batlló

46 ☆ On reaching Carrer Aragó, turn left to find **EDITORIAL MONTANER I SIMÓN** (MONTANER I SIMÓN EDITOR'S), a publishing company owned by the family of Domènech i Montaner's mother, which currently houses the **FUNDACIÓ ANTONI TÀPIES**. Built by Domènech i Montaner himself from 1881 to 1886, this is one of the pioneering examples of the architectural and urban renovation that was introduced by the Modernista movement, together with Gaudí's Casa Vicens (number **(88)** of the Modernisme Route). The building features a very unacademic façade with a slightly Mudejar (Moorish) appearance, a system of skylights that provides very diffuse top lighting, and a peculiar structure with cast iron pillars and steel beams that is more characteristic of markets and railway stations of the of the late

Editorial Montaner i Simón - Fundació Antoni Tàpies

Address	Aragó, 255.
Open	Daily except Mondays, 10am to 8pm. CLosed on January 1st and 6th and December 25th and 26th.
Information	Tel.: 934 870 315. www.fundaciotapies.org
Further details	Timetables may change. Check updates and information on Route discount at **www.rutadelmodernisme.com** or call tel.: 902 076 621.

19th century. The building is now crowned by a sculptural work by the great contemporary artist Antoni Tàpies, *Núvol i cadira (Cloud and Chair)*, which has become the emblem of his foundation. The museum exhibits a wide selection of the work of this Catalan artist and holds temporary exhibitions, symposia, conferences and film cycles. It also houses a library specialised in modern and contemporary art, the Tàpies archive with the largest collection of his works and related documents, and collections on Asian and Pre-Columbine arts and culture.

→ page 86

Editorial Montaner i Simón

On this point we may take a detour from the main One-day Route to reach Rambla Catalunya, where on the left we will see **CASA DOLORS CALM** (DOLORS CALM HOUSE. Rambla de Catalunya, 54). This building, remodelled in 1903 by Josep Vilaseca i Casanovas, features **47**

Casa Dolors Calm

Casa Fargas

elegant -if rather deteriorated- marquetry on the set of bay windows on the façades, sgraffito work, and sculptural elements on the ground floor and the cornice. A few metres away on the opposite side of the avenue is **CASA FARGAS** (FARGAS HOUSE. Rambla Catalunya, 47) by Enric Sagnier (1902-1904). Its most outstanding element, the dome, disappeared during a later addition of floors, and the main interest at present lies in the sober design of the undulating bay windows. Now continue down Rambla Catalunya and turn right at Carrer Diputació, where you will find another **48**

Casa Garriga Nogués

49 building by Sagnier built in the same years as Casa Fargas, the **CASA GARRIGA NOGUÉS** (GARRIGA NOGUÉS HOUSE. Diputació, 250), which features corbels by Eusebi Arnau representing the ages of man, and stained glass windows on the piano nobile. Turning back into Rambla
50 de Catalunya, a little further up on the same side is the **FARMÀCIA BOLÓS** (BOLOS PHARMACY. Rambla de Catalunya, 77) by Josep Domènech i Estapà, built between 1904 and 1910, which still has almost all its original decorative elements: a presumptuous, aristocratic lamp bearing the name of the shop, a stained glass window depicting an orange tree, and furniture, all designed by the great craftsman Antoni Falguera. A little further up, on the

Farmàcia Bolós

opposite side of the street, you will come to **CASA DOMÈNECH I ESTAPÀ** (DOMÈNECH I ESTAPÀ HOUSE. València, 241), built by the architect Josep Domènech i Estapà for his own family in 1908-1909, which features a curious asymmetric distribution of the exposed masonry façade with a bay window on one side offset by a line of windows on the other. 51

Casa Domènech i Estapà

If you return to Rambla de Catalunya, a little further up on the same side you will come to the **CASA JUNCOSA** (JUNCOSA HOUSE. Rambla Catalunya, 78), by Salvador Viñals i Sabaté (1907-1909), which occupies a large site on the corner of Carrer València and features a large central bay window and a slightly Modernista foyer. On the corner of Carrer 52

Casa Juncosa

53 Mallorca stands the **CASA QUERALTÓ** (QUERALTÓ HOUSE. Rambla Catalunya, 88), a 1907 building by Josep Plantada i Artigas which has undergone major modifications in the course of time, including the mutilation of its crown. It is decorated with elegant pink sgraffito work and false arches with columns and capitals.

Casa Queraltó

If you now return to Passeig de Gràcia, slightly further up at the corner of Carrer

54 València you will find the **CASA VÍDUA MARFÀ** (MARFÀ HOUSE. Passeig de Gràcia, 66), one of the best examples of the Neo-Medieval style language imported by Modernista architects. Built by Manuel Comas i Thos between 1901 and 1905, it features three

Casa Vídua Marfà

semicircular arches giving onto the street and slender columns supporting the bay window on the façade. On the corner opposite the Casa Marfà is the Hotel Majestic and just in front of it you can see one of the 31 **BANCS/FANALS** (BENCHES/STREET LAMPS) designed in 1906 by Pere Falqués to light the ostentatious boulevard appropriately. Restored from their then very deteriorated state in the 1980s by the City Council, one must distinguish these original elements from the circular benches-cum-flower beds you will find on some of the wide chamfers of Passeig de Gràcia. 55

They are the fruit of a certain contemporary "Neo-Modernisme" and were added to the avenue's landscape at the end of the 20th century, their suitability still being challenged today. → page 94

A major detour from the main route, turning right at Carrer València, takes you to the **CASA ELIZALDE** (ELIZALDE HOUSE. València, 302), a house built in 1885 for the Sala family that currently houses a municipal civic centre. (From here Modernisme itineraries are organised on Saturday mornings. These must be booked in advance. For further information, phone 934 880 590). The building is of limited architectural interest, but features a monumental court. At the corner of Carrer València and Carrer Roger
56 de Llúria you will find the popular **QUEVIURES MÚRRIA** (MÚRRIA GROCERY. Roger de Llúria, 85), a historic commercial establishment that opened in 1898 as a coffee roaster and rolled wafer manufacturer under the name of a nearby church, "La Puríssima". The shop evolved to become one of the most famous Barcelona groceries, and features Modernista fire-tinted glazing signs that bring a cheerful touch to the façade, in particular the original advertisement for Anís del Mono, designed by Ramon Casas.

Queviures Múrria

Casa Josefa Villanueva

A short distance away are three Modernista buildings of interest. **CASA JOSEFA VILLANUEVA** (JOSEFA VILLANUEVA HOUSE. València, 312), built between 1904 and 1909 by Juli M. Fossas, features an elegant bay window on one of the corners that formerly had its counterpart, now disappeared, on the other corner of the building. Across the street is **CASA JAUME FORN** (JAUME FORN HOUSE. València, 285), a building by Jeroni F. Granell i Manresa dating from 1909 with striking stained glass bay windows at the corners, 57 58

Casa Jaume Forn

though a later addition of floors distorted the original work. Nearby,
59 **CASA SANTURCE** (SANTURCE HOUSE. València, 293) by Miquel Madorell i Rius (1902-1905), which has an interesting foyer and a façade decorated with two strikingly crowned bay windows and a coat of arms with the name of the owner, the Count of San José de Santurce.

Walk a little further along Carrer València and you will come to the building of the
☆ 60 **CONSERVATORI MUNICIPAL DE MÚSICA** (MUNICIPAL CONSERVATORY OF MUSIC. Bruc, 104-112), designed in 1916-1928 at the

Casa Santurce - Casa Pau Ubarri

Conservatori Municipal de Música

end of the "Modernista fever" by Antoni de Falguera, a specialist in municipal buildings.
61 Going up Carrer Girona is **CASA LAMADRID** (LAMADRID HOUSE. Girona, 113), built by Lluís Domènech i Montaner in 1902. Although it may be considered a relatively simple house considering the author, it does have a particularly interesting façade, a compendium of the traditional decorative repertory of its designer, with a striking sculptural crown decorated
62 with plant motifs and a Gothic-style coat of arms. On the other side of the street, the **CASA GRANELL** (GRANELL HOUSE. Girona, 122) is an excellent example of the simpler Modernista style that was used in dwellings of less well-off people, a modest building of which Jeroni F. Granell i Manresa was both architect (1901-1903) and owner.

Casa Lamadrid

Casa Granell

Returning to Carrer València, a little further along you will come to the **CASA LLOPIS BOFILL** (LLOPIS BOFILL HOUSE. València, 339 / Bailèn, 113), perhaps the most outstanding work by Antoni M. Gallissà (1902). This large building, which has undergone major modifications, is a showcase of decorative details that are clearly influenced by Domènech i Montaner. Particularly outstanding are the extraordinary ground floor and the bay windows and balconies of the façade. 63

Casa Llopis Bofill

Casa Vallet i Xiró

If you go up Carrer Bailèn you will come to Carrer Mallorca. Along this street you will go past the **FARMÀCIA PUIGORIOL** (PUIGORIOL PHARMACY. Mallorca, 312), an establishment with Modernista decoration. Then walk towards Passeig de Gràcia and you will come to
64 the **CASA VALLET I XIRÓ** (VALLET I XIRÓ HOUSE. Mallorca, 302), by the architect Josep M. Barenys i Gambús, dating from 1913 and considered to be late Modernista in style, with
☆ 65 Central European Secession influences. Further along you will come to **CASA THOMAS** (THOMAS HOUSE. Mallorca, 291-293), designed by Domènech i Montaner. The main interest of this building, built between 1895 and 1898, is that it shows the first characteristic signs of this architect's unmistakeable style, such as the Neo-Gothic façade, the bluish tones and the foyer featuring floral motifs with figures of reptiles. The house that can be seen today is not, however, the first design by Domènech i Montaner. The building was originally limited to the workshop and the first floor, the dwelling of the owner. When it was extended in 1912 the original lines were respected, the towers were rebuilt at a higher level and elegant bay windows were added to the façade.

Casa Thomas

A litlle bit further on, on the corner with Carrer Llúria is the **PALAU MONTANER**, completed by a young Domènech i Montaner in 1896 for one of the owners of the Montaner i Simon publishing firm -though the building was begun by Josep Domènech i Estapà until he resigned in 1891 after an argument with the owner, leaving two stories

Palau Montaner

Address	Mallorca, 278.
Open	Only for guided visits, some Saturdays and Sundays at 10.30 and 11.30am, and at 12.30pm.
Information	Tel.: 902 076 621. www.rutadelmodernisme.com
Further details	Timetables and language of visits may change without prior notice due to security reasons. Check updates and information on Route discount at **www.rutadelmodernisme.com** or call 902 076 621.

Palau Montaner

already standing. Decorative elements related to the art of printing can be found both inside and outside, but the interior is especially exquisite. Here we find the stamp of great artists of Modernisme, like the sculptor Eusebi Arnau, the carpenter Gaspar Homar and the glassmaker Antoni Rigalt. The mansion is richly decorated, with mosaics, sculptures, carved woodwork and a spectacular staircase under a grand ornamental glass skylight. The palace is now is one of the headquarters of the Madrid Government's Delegation in Catalonia. On the opposite corner is the **PALAU CASADES** (Mallorca, 283), a Pompeian mansion designed by Antoni Serra i Pujals (1885) and featuring an unusual court decorated with polychrome columns. Since 1922 this has been the College of Lawyers centre. From here, the route returns to Passeig de Gràcia.

Back on Passeig de Gràcia, almost beside Hotel Majestic, is **CASA JOAN COMAS** (Passeig de Gràcia, 74), in which Enric Sagnier (1907) undertook a thorough remodelling of an existing building, modifying its rear balconies, converting the garden into a warehouse, and giving the façade a Modernista appearance by adding a bay window, new railings on the balconies, and a curved cornice. Nevertheless, the building is considered to be predominantly eclectic in style. A little further up, at the crossroads of Carrer Mallorca, on the other side of the avenue is the Neo-Gothic inspired **CASA ENRIC BATLLÓ** (Passeig de Gràcia, 75), designed by Josep Vilaseca i Casanovas (1895-1896), which today houses a hotel and has one of the most attractive façades on the Passeig, thanks to its brilliant polychromy. Crossing Passeig de Gràcia and going up to the corner of Carrer Provença, you will come to the jewel in the crown of Modernisme in Barcelona, standing majestically over the intersection.

Until 1905, on this corner there stood a modest three-storey building with a garden. After its demolition it was replaced by one of Gaudí's most admired and photographed works: **CASA MILÀ**, popularly known as **LA PEDRERA**. The last residential building by Gaudí, it was built between 1906 and 1910 for Pere Milà, a property developer married to Rosario Segimón, the widow of José Guardiola, a wealthy *Indiano* (as Catalans returning rich from the American colonies were called). Milà was a young and successful businessman who indulged in luxury, novelty and fashion, a true dandy of Modernista Bacelona. He was one of the first to boast a private motor car in the city's avenues, and as he went by Barcelonans joked about his love of money and opulence, wondering if he wasn't rather more interested in "the widow's *guardiola*" (piggy bank), than in "Guardiola's widow".

67

Casa Milà - La Pedrera

Address	Passeig de Gràcia, 92 / Provença, 261-265.
Open	Daily 10am to 8pm (last admission 7.30pm). Closed on January 1st and 6th and December 25th and 26th.
Information	Tel.: 902 400 973. www.fundaciocaixacatalunya.org
Further details	Timetables may vary. Check updates and information on Route discount at **www.rutadelmodernisme.com** or call 902 076 621.

Fully swinging in the Modernista "fever", Milà decided to commission a building that would outdo the illustrious neighbours (Casa Batlló, Casa Amatller and Casa Lleó Morera). And indeed he achieved it. Inspired by an unlimited budget, Gaudí regaled the city with a geological landscape, a sea cliff, an abstract sculpture with giant organic forms. The Casa Milà is in fact the definitive triumph of the curved line, imposing in this work as never before. La Pedrera (The Quarry) is the name that the people of Barcelona gave the building when they saw it completed in 1910 and were amazed at the revolutionary and bizarre façade which led to many popular jokes and criticism by cartoonists and writers. The painter Santiago Rusiñol, for example, joked that nobody who lived in La Pedrera could have a dog or cat -their pet would have to be a snake! After a visit to Barcelona, the French politician Georges Clemenceau also remarked that the Catalans were so inspired by the legend of Saint George that they even built houses for dragons. Cartoonists portrayed it as a garage for airships or a cliff full of caves infested with animals. Others likened it to the newspaper images of a recent earthquake in Andalusia.

Gaudí did not conceive the Casa Milà as a simple residential building, but as a complete work that ventured from architecture into the realm of sculpture. The façade, influenced by the early international Art Nouveau movement, is clad in limestone blocks that were rough-hewn to achieve a matte finish, forming characteristic curved volumes and sinuous arabesques that recall a sea cliff with cave dwellings marked by evocatively shaped wrought iron balconies. The lower part of the façade is built with stone from the Garraf Massif and the upper part with stone from Vilafranca del Penedès, both

south of Barcelona. Originally, Gaudí aimed to convert La Pedrera into a religious allegory of the Holy Rosary, culminating atop the façade with a four-metre-high bronze medallion. However, the Setmana Tràgica (Tragic Week, a social revolt sparked in 1909 by the mobilisation of the Catalan reservists to fight in Morocco, during which churches were attacked and burnt) persuaded Milà that a residential dwelling with a giant virgin on the terrace would undoubtedly become the next target for anti-clerical mobs. He therefore quietly cancelled this part of the scheme.

Casa Milà - Piano nobile

Some claim that the interior layout of La Pedrera was taken from Gaudí's studies of medieval fortresses. This image is reinforced by the chimneys and accesses to the roof terrace that look like sentinels with helmets. The interior, however, is nothing like a fortress. The paintings on the ceilings of the foyers and the inner courts are particularly interesting. From the foyers one can enter the old underground coach house, now converted into a sloping, semicircular auditorium with wrought iron and brick columns supporting the building (not

Casa Milà - Courtyard

included in the visit). Milà's wife, Rosario Segimón, never shared her husband's devotion to Gaudí but acquiesced to living in a Gaudinian space until 1926 when, after the architect's death, she decided to redecorate the main floor in a Louis XVI style that was far more to her taste. After the removal of the dividing walls, this space is now used for the large exhibitions organised by the Caixa Catalunya Foundation, present owner of the building.

Casa Milà - Attic vaults

On the top floor of the building is the attic, which now houses the Gaudí Space, and has been restored to the appearance that it had when it was designed by Gaudí. Built in brick, it originally housed the washrooms of the house. The ground plan is a wide figure of eight, and it has 270 parabolic arches that years later captured the imagination of Le Corbusier and -according to the mood of the visitor- can be seen as the ribs of an immense animal or as a palm tree. The recovery of this space involved the removal of 13 apartments built in 1953: although these apartments did have their architectural interest, they had hidden one of the secrets of this part of the house.

Casa Milà - Chimneys

When it was returned to its original state, it was found that Gaudí had given a logical order to the small windows distributed at different levels to allow light and a constant current of air into the attic, which was also designed for drying laundry. The Gaudí Space currently attempts to illustrate the personality of the architect through a series of drawings, models, photographs and audio-visual materials that explain his life, his historical and cultural context, and the artistic values and technical innovations of his work.

From the Gaudí Space, there is access to the stepped roof terrace of la Pedrera, which the poet Pere Gimferrer called a "warriors' garden". The roof terrace has also undergone a radical restoration: only Gaudí's original chimneys have been maintained, now returned to their splendour together with the stairwells, clad with fragments of marble and *trencadís* of Valencia tiles. The one chimney which is crowned with glass bottle fragments was restored with champagne bottle bottoms from the turn of the 20th century (according to hearsay Gaudí designed this by using the empties on the morning after the inauguration party). The work of the restorers has recovered the original force of the Ulldecona stone overhang decorated with fragments of floor tiles. Though the overall colour is cream, this area is more multi-coloured than the grey-white façade. The six exits from the stairwells punctuate this world-famous roof terrace. From here one can see a different perspective of the inner courts of the Casa Milà and, at the distance rising from the cityscape, the Sagrada Família.

The last stage of the visit to La Pedrera is "El Pis de La Pedrera" a space that shows the key elements of Gaudí's architecture and gives the visitors an idea of the lifestyle of a bourgeois family in Barcelona in the early 20th century. This space occupies two former dwellings of La Pedrera, covering almost 600 square metres, and provides a total reconstruction of the period, including the typical study room, the old bathrooms and the small servants' quarters.

Casa Milà was listed World Heritage by UNESCO in 1984. Curiously enough, in the early 1980s the appearance of the Casa Milà was deplorable. The façade was a dark brown colour, the frescoes in the foyer were seriously deteriorated, the main floor had been transformed into a bingo hall, and the shops on the ground floor did not respect the curves of the original openings. After the restoration, the gloomy building recovered all its splendour. At present, the building is the headquarters of the Caixa Catalunya Foundation. The savings bank Caixa Catalunya has since 1986 invested more than 48 million euros in its restoration, which has involved the repair of the serious mutilations that the building had undergone, the restoration of the original appearance of the attic and roof terrace, and the recovery of the original paint colours of the inner courts, which had suffered damage ranging from destruction during the Civil War to the slow but sure effects of pollution. The corridors linking the courts and the inner staircases have also been restored to the original apple green colour that Gaudí gave them.

Leaving La Pedrera, we continue up Passeig de Gràcia towards Avinguda Diagonal. After a few metres we find the **CASA CASAS-CARBÓ** (Passeig de Gràcia, 96), built by Antoni Rovira i Rabassa in 1894. The main interest of this building, which was the residence of the painter Ramon Casas and the writer Santiago Rusiñol, is its interior which features the terrace of the main floor, an elegant Romantic garden of the late 19th century, and the fireplace designed by the decorator Josep Pascó (1902) for the piano nobile of the building. The only outstanding 68

Casa Casas-Carbó

feature on the façade is the carved stone balcony of the main floor. The last important building before reaching Avinguda Diagonal is **PALAU ROBERT** (Passeig de Gràcia, 107), a noble building surrounded by gardens built in 1903 in Neo-Classical style. This building, by Henri Grandpierre and Joan Martorell i Montells, was a private residence until 1981, when it was acquired by the Generalitat of Catalonia, to house its tourist information offices.

The intersection of Avinguda Diagonal and Passeig de Gràcia is popularly known as Cinc d'Oros -the "five of gold coins" from the Spanish-style pack of cards- because of the five Modernista lamp-posts by Falqués that decorated the square at the beginning of the 20th century (they are now on Avinguda Gaudí, between the Sagrada Família **(81)** and Hospital de Sant Pau **(82)**). The intersection is currently presided by an obelisk which used to support a statue of the Republic by Josep Viladomat, withdrawn after the Civil War (and currently relocated in Plaça Llucmajor, in the northern area of Barcelona). The substitute statue at the base of the obelisk, dedicated to the fascist Victory of 1939, was made by Frederic Marès, although with the advent of democracy in 1979 the fascist symbols adorning it were erased by the Barcelona City Council, as with many other monuments and buildings in town. -› page 103

69 Along Avinguda Diagonal, west towards Plaça Francesc Macià, you will come to **CASA**

Casa Serra

SERRA (Rambla de Catalunya, 126), which in its time was one of the best examples of single-family urban mansions in Barcelona. The building, planned by Josep Puig i Cadafalch in 1903, is now backed by a contemporary building with a glass façade which Antoni Milà and Frederic Correa built in 1987. This daring combination of Modernisme and modern design now houses the Provincial Council of Barcelona. Of the original design, two wings forming an angle give onto Rambla Catalunya: in one of them there is a Plateresque door in which Puig i Cadafalch emulated the door of the Casa Gralla, a Renaissance building demolished in 1856 in Carrer Portaferrisa. The Eclecticism of the architect seems to have no limits in this work. In addition to the Plateresque door, the balconies and windows combine Gothic and Renaissance elements.

Casa Antoni Costa

At this point it is worth remembering that only one block from here, at the crossroads of Carrer Balmes and Carrer Còrsega, was the **Casa Trinxet**, another work by Josep Puig i Cadafalch (this one from 1902-1904) that is no longer standing. It had a spectacular interior, but was demolished in 1968 despite attempts by artists and intellectuals to save it for conversion into a museum of Modernisme. Very close to Casa Serra is
CASA ANTONI COSTA (Rambla de 70
Catalunya, 122), perhaps the most representative multi-family dwelling by Josep Domènech i Estapà (1904), a monumentalist building with Secession influences. Further along Avinguda Diagonal, presiding over the corner of
Carrer Enric Granados, is the **CASA** 71
SAYRACH (Diagonal, 423-425), one of the most outstanding examples of late Barcelona Modernisme. Built in 1918, the house is unique because of the curved forms of the façade, in which the influence of Gaudí may clearly be seen, and because of the slender tower at the corner. The entrance hall is an apotheosis of the most Baroque Modernisme. This work is now attributed to the architect and writer Manuel Sayrach i Carreras, even if the

Casa Sayrach

project was signed by Gabriel Borrell. If you now go down Carrer Enric Granados and follow Carrer Paris toward the right, you will come to the intersection with Carrer Aribau and the **CASA SOCIETAT TORRES GERMANS** (Aribau, 180), a building by Jaume Torres (1906) featuring sets of bay windows at the ends of the façade, sgraffito work and a stepped cornice.

72 Back on Avinguda Diagonal, at the crossroads with Carrer Buenos Aires is the **CASA PERE COMPANY**. The house was proposed for the Barcelona City Council prize for the best building in 1911, though this was finally awarded to the Casaramona factory **(35)** by the same architect. The building is considered the first of Puig's "white period", in which the architect introduced influences from the Viennese Secession in his projects. On the façade some decorative elements have been maintained, such as the sgraffito work by Tomás Fontanals on the façade facing Carrer Buenos Aires, depicting Our Lady of the Assumption. In 1940, the building was purchased by a famous gynaecologist, doctor Melcior Colet Torrebadella, who converted it into a clinic. The work was carried out under the direction of the interior designer Santiago Marco Urrutia (1885-1949), who transformed the house interior and only preserved the original fireplace by Puig i Cadafalch. In 1982, Doctor Colet gave the building to the Generalitat's Directorate-General for Sports for conversion into the current museum.

Casa Pere Company - Museu de l'Esport	
Address	Buenos Aires, 56-58
Open	Daily except Sundays and holidays, 10am to 2pm and 4pm to 7pm
Information	Tel.: 934 192 232 http://cultura.gencat.net/esport/colet/index.htm
Further details	Timetables may vary. Check updates and information on Route discount at **www.rutadelmodernisme.com** or call 902 076 621

Casa Company

Casa Pérez Samanillo

Back at the Cinc d'Oros, on the opposite side is the **CASA PÉREZ SAMANILLO** (Diagonal, 502-504), the headquarters of the Círculo Eqüestre, a high-society club. Built in 1910 by Joan Josep Hervàs i Arizmendi, the house has undergone many modifications in the course of history. One of the main original features of this Neo-Gothic style mansion is the oval window of the dining room that gives onto Avinguda Diagonal, popularly known as "the fish tank". A few steps further along is the façade of the **POMPEIA CHURCH** (Diagonal, 450), a Neo-Gothic church that Enric Sagnier i Villavechia designed in 1909 for the Capuchin fathers, whose main features are the exterior façade of red brick and stone and the stained glass of the entrance. 73

Above the Cinc d'Oros, Passeig de Gràcia becomes a landscaped space that the inhabitants of the Gràcia district call 'Els Jardinets' (The Little Gardens). This small green is a miniature open-air museum of sculptures: a metal installation and the sculpture *La Lectura (Reading)* by Josep Clarà are homage to Pompeu Fabra, author of the modern Catalan grammatical rules. This final section of Passeig de Gràcia, between Avinguda Diagonal and the urban fabric of the old town of Gràcia, has two outstanding Modernista buildings. One of them is the **CASA BONAVENTURA FERRER** (Passeig de Gràcia, 113), 74
built by Pere Falqués in 1906. Falqués gave a striking sculptural treatment to the façade

Casa Bonaventura Ferrer

of this building, particularly in the bay window, which gives it an exceptionally monumental appearance. Slightly further up is the **CASA FUSTER** (Passeig de Gràcia, 132) Domènech i Montaner's last work in Barcelona (1908-1911). This building marks the end of Passeig de Gràcia and to some extent summarises the work of Lluís Domènech i Montaner. The façade has a cylindrical tower typical of the architect, adorned with sculptures that simulate swallows' nests, and a curious French-style attic which is not very common in Modernista architecture. The building should have been crowned with a tower similar to that of the administration pavilion of the Hospital de Sant Pau, but it was never completed.

☆ 75

Casa Fuster

Casa Fuster - Façade, and inside the Cafè Vienès

For many years, the mythical Cafè Vienès wich occupied the ground floor, together with the dance hall El Danubio in the basement, was one of the main meeting points of the city. In 2004 the company Hoteles Center reopened the Cafè Vienès, after buying the house and fully restoring it into a luxury hotel (for further information see *Let's Go Out*, the guide to Modernista bars and restaurants).

Back on Avinguda Diagonal, going towards Passeig de Sant Joan, the Route comes to a building by Josep Puig i Cadafalch, the **PALAU DEL BARÓ DE QUADRAS** (Diagonal, 373). Built in 1904, it is now the premises of the House of Asia (Casa Àsia, tel. 932 387 337, www.casaasia.es), a public institution set up in 2001 with the aim of promoting actions and projects to foster development with Asia in the institutional, cultural, academic and economic spheres. The mansion is a veritable compendium of Puig i Cadafalch's capacity for design and elegance. Everything is exemplary: from the wrought iron door to the interior, with a highly ornamented foyer. One of the curiosities is the building's double façade. The façade giving onto Avinguda Diagonal emphasises the noble nature of the mansion, and combines Gothic and Plateresque forms with an abundant floral decoration. The rear façade (giving onto Carrer Rosselló) reveals that the building was in origin not a palace, but a simple block of flats. The Arabic-style interior contains Roman mosaics, polychrome woodwork, sgraffito work and wooden lattices. 76 ☆

Palau del Baró de Quadras - Courtyard

Palau del Baró de Quadras - Casa Àsia

Address	Diagonal, 373.
Open	Monday to Friday 10am to 8pm, Saturdays 10am to 2pm Exhibitions: Tuesday to Saturday 10am to 8pm, Sundays and holidays 10am to 2pm.Closed on December 24th, 25th, 26th and 31st and January 1st and 2nd
Information	Tel. 932 387 337. www.casaasia.es
Further details	Timetables may vary. Check updates and information on Route discount at **www.rutadelmodernisme.com** or call 902 076 621

Casa Comalat - Rear façade

On the opposite side of the avenue is the **CASA COMALAT** (Diagonal, 442) by Salvador Valeri i Popurull. This unusual and spectacular work (1909-1911), which is highly influenced by Gaudí, is also particularly interesting for its two façades: the main façade, which is symmetrical and urban, and the rear façade (on Carrer Còrsega), which is less formal, polychrome and decorated with peculiar Modernista wooden galleries with blinds and coloured ceramic work. The interior is no less impressive, with mosaic paving and exquisite furniture featuring unusually shaped benches and the peculiar foyer lights. 77 ☆

On the same side of Avinguda Diagonal, at the intersection with Carrer Rosselló and Carrer Roger de Llúria, is the **CASA TERRADES** (Diagonal, 416-420). This imposing building, known popularly as **CASA DE LES PUNXES** (HOUSE OF THE SPIRES), was built in 1905 by Josep Puig i Cadafalch on a large site owned by the Terrades sisters. With a striking and characteristic silhouette, Casa de les Punxes is one of the most famous Modernista works. Though it seems to be a uniform block, it is in fact composed of three apartment houses. In its construction, Puig i Cadafalch exaggerated his highly stylised traditional medieval elements to the point that the building looks like a castle. It has four round towers crowned by conical turrets, a main tower with a dome and a host of bay windows and belvederes in Flamboyant Gothic style. The Australian writer Robert Hughes described it in his book *Barcelona* as "a cross between a Flemish guildhall and a medievalising Mad Ludwig (referring to Louis 2nd, King of Bavaria) schloss". Its spectacular façade is clad in brick, except on the ground floor where stone is used, and it features wrought iron work, balconies and ceramic panels 78 ☆

Casa Terrades

Casa Terrades

depicting patriotic motifs. One of these, the largest and best-known, represents Saint George and proudly bears the following legend: "Sant Patró de Catalunya, torneu-nos la llibertat" ("Holy Patron of Catalonia, give us back our freedom") which at the time was considered by some to be a provocation. The fiery politician Alejandro Lerroux called it "a crime against the nation" (the Spanish nation, in this case), but art prevailed over politics and the panel was preserved -even during fascism and with a police station in front of it!

Continuing along Avinguda Diagonal we come to Plaça Mossèn Jacint Verdaguer, presided over by a monument to Verdaguer, the nineteenth-century "National Poet of Catalonia". The monument was designed in 1914 by a Josep M. Pericas that was already evolving, moving away from Modernisme: the statue is by Joan Borrell, and the stone reliefs by the ☆ 79 Oslé brothers. From this square one can see the **CASA MACAYA** (Passeig de Sant Joan, 108), an urban residence built by Josep Puig i Cadafalch in 1901. This mansion is another medievalistic experiment by the Catalan architect. The white façade of the palace, culminating in two side turrets, has sgraffito work and openings with sculptural decoration, including

Casa Macaya

capitals by Eusebi Arnau depicting very contemporary subjects, such as the cyclist beside the main door. The highly ornamental decoration of the interior has almost all been lost except for the foyer, decorated with sgraffito work and tiles, and the courtyard with an open staircase in the purest style of the medieval mansions of Barcelona.

Returning to the Diagonal and going east towards Plaça de les Glòries we find, at the corner of Carrer Sicilia, the **CASA PLANELLS** (Diagonal, 332), an original building of rounded forms built in 1924 80 ☆

Casa Planells

by Josep Maria Jujol i Gibert, a student of Gaudí. Many specialists consider this house as the last Modernista work in Barcelona, but the influence of new avant-garde and rationalist trends is evident. Jujol did an admirable job of using a small site to design maisonettes connected by interior spiral stairs.

Going up Carrer Sicilia and turning right at Carrer Mallorca we reach the **TEMPLE EXPIATORI DE LA SAGRADA FAMÍLIA** (EXPIATORY TEMPLE OF THE HOLY FAMILY). Gaudí was a unique architect in his time, and one of the few in the history of architecture to have had a commission that lasted a lifetime -in fact, a commission that outlived him. The Sagrada Família is a work of great brilliance and ambition and of giant aspirations. 81 ☆

Temple Expiatori de la Sagrada Família

Address	Mallorca, 401
Open	All year round except January 1st and 6th and December 25th and 26th. October to March, 9am to 6pm; April to September 9am to 8pm
Information	Tel.: 932 080 414. www.sagradafamilia.org
Further details	Timetables may vary. Check updates and information on Route discount at **www.rutadelmodernisme.com** or call 902 076 621

The origin of the Expiatory Church of the Holy Family dates back to 1869 when Josep M. Bocabella, founder of the Josephite Association dedicated to fostering devotion to Saint Joseph, had the idea of building a church to honour the Holy Family (Saint Joseph, the Virgin Mary and Jesus Christ). Bocabella bought a site and in 1882 started to build a church in a Neo-Gothic style with the aim of creating a cathedral for the poor, to counteract the anticlerical radicalism that was beginning to spread among the lower classes of Barcelona (the city anarchist leader Mikhail Bakunin had pointed out as the most revolutionary in all of Europe). However, in the course of time the church took on a very different meaning as conservative Catalan nationalists began to identify with the project. The initial design of the church was by Francesc de Paula Villar, but the lack of understanding between the owner

Sagrada Família - Spiral staircase

and the architect led to a radical change of plans. Villar was dismissed and replaced by Antoni Gaudí, who finished the crypt and presented a new, far more ambitious plan: to build a cathedral with a great, central, 170-metre-high tower dedicated to the Saviour. Pious Mr. Bocabella was thrilled with the idea and Gaudí plunged into the project. Progress, however, was not easy. In 1891 he started work on the Nativity façade: thirty-four years later, in 1925, Gaudí had finished only the first of the four bell towers that crown this façade. The other three were finished after the death of the architect.

The Sagrada Família may be considered a Bible in stone, owing to the great number of Christian symbols that Gaudí placed on its façades. These include, or rather will include once finished, Adam and Eve, the Twelve Apostles, all the episodes of the life of Jesus and all the main symbols of the Old Testament. The Sagrada Família is, indeed, a monument that could be used as an introductory crash-course to Catholic religion. The importance of this building is not, however, exclusively religious. It is also the "book of Gaudí", the clearest lesson of his way of building, a kind of testament in which Gaudí applied all the structural solutions that he had studied and tested in his different works. The work where he paid his last homage to nature, which he called "the best builder" and which he always strove to imitate. One can see this clearly in the way the

church is supported on leaning columns whose branches support small hyperboloid sections of vault, producing the effect of a forest.

The Nativity Façade, on Carrer Marina, is Gaudí's great work. Almost completed by the architect, it attempts to express and communicate the joy of creation through the birth of Jesus. In the central archivolt, one can see Jesus, Joseph and Mary under the Star of Bethlehem and with the ox and the mule, surrounded by angels, musicians and singers. A careful examination of the façade's decoration reveals over a hundred plant species and a hundred animals sculpted on the archivolts and ribs. This façade has three doors. The central one is the Door of Charity, inscribed with the names of the genealogy of Christ, from the beginning of the snake with the apple to the baby Jesus with the ox and the mule, and the signs of the Zodiac as they were on the day of Christ's birth. On the south side is the Door of Hope, representing the marriage of Joseph and Mary, the flight to Egypt, the massacre of the innocents and a representation of the Montserrat mountain with the inscription "Salveu-nos" ("Save us": Montserrat Mountain is traditionally considered a holy mountain and the Virgin of Montserrat the patron of Catalonia). On the opposite side is the Door of Faith representing the scenes of the Visitation; Jesus among the wise men in the temple and at his carpenter's bench. The pinnacles of this façade resemble ears of corn and bunches of grapes, presided by the image of Mary as the Immaculate Conception. The façade as a whole celebrates the triumph of life.

The Passion Façade on Carrer Sardenya is the counterpoint to the Nativity Façade. This façade includes over a hundred contemporary sculptures evoking the Passion by the sculptor Josep Maria Subirachs. Desolation, nudity, pain and sacrifice all accompany the death of Christ to announce his resurrection and ascent to heaven. Gaudí often repeated that, had he started with this façade, people would have rejected the Sagrada Familia outright. In contrast with the decorated, ornamented and turgid Nativity Façade, the Passion Door is harsh and naked, as if it were made of bones. Through a larger portico supported by six large leaning columns as sequoia tree trunks, an immense pediment rises with 18 smaller columns supporting an inner portico. The lack of decoration concentrates the tragedy in the dramatic main events, presided by the naked figure of Christ at the moment of his death.

The main façade, which will represent the life and destiny of man, is still to be built. According to Gaudí's plan, it will face the sea looking over Carrer Mallorca, which would be covered by a large plaza reached by a huge staircase rising from what today is the doomed block of houses facing the temple. What is beginning to take shape is totally new forms in the naves of the church, which show unusual geometrical and structural solutions. The naves of the church are the result of years of study and reflection: it wasn't until 1910 that Gaudí started the study of the naves, incorporating the experience he had acquired in the chapel of the Colònia Güell. However, the discovery of the luminosity of the hyperboloid led Gaudí to use concave-convex domes fitted to columns, walls and windows. At a scale of 1/10, this was the vision of the forest that he often used to explain his design.

Sagrada Família - The Schools in the 1950's

The museum of the church conserves the history of its construction in site plans, photographs of different periods of the construction, fragments of models, iconography and wrought iron, wood and metal work designed by Gaudí, in addition to photographs and an audiovisual presentation on other buildings by the same architect. One can also see the models of the central nave and the façades. The most outstanding exhibits are the model that was used to calculate the structure of the church of the Colònia Güell (a solution including slightly helicoidal columns and paraboloid-helicoid arches) and a score of original drawings by the architect. There are also photographs of other buildings by Gaudí and elements that he designed and that were modelled in the workshops of the church. One of the adjoining facilities is the Sagrada Família Schools, a simple curvilinear building with the stamp of Gaudí that dazzled Le Corbusier with its technical boldness. These schools, originally intended for the children of the builders who were working on the site, form an innovative building in which Gaudí did not use iron and made all the structures with brick, thus achieving great plasticity with a very cheap material.

From the Nativity Façade of the Sagrada Família, on Carrer Marina, one can see the start of Avinguda Gaudí, adorned with a sculpture by Apel·les Fenosa and the old Modernista street lamps by Pere Falqués which used to stand at the the Cinc d'Oros, on the crossing of Diagonal with Passeig de Gràcia. Avinguda Gaudí leads to the **HOSPITAL DE LA SANTA CREU I SANT PAU** (HOSPITAL OF THE HOLY CROSS AND OF SAINT PAUL) wich stands at the opposite end of the avenue. Construction of the current premises began in 1902, following a design by Lluís Domènech i Montaner, who was sensitive to the new hygienist theories of public health applied to town planning promoted by the doctor Pere Felip Monlau and engineers Ildefons Cerdà and Pere García Faria (designer of the Barcelona underground sewage network in the 19th century). The new hospital was raised on one of the ends of the Eixample district, on land bought by the Hospital de la Santa Creu thanks to a donation by the banker Pau Gil. Gil provided in his will for the construction of a health centre bearing his Christian name, and thus "Sant Pau" was added to the "Santa Creu". 82 ☆

Hospital de la Santa Creu i Sant Pau - Modernisme Centre

Address	Sant Antoni Maria Claret, 167
Open	Daily from 10am to 2pm (last visit at 1.30pm) Closed on January 1st and 6th and December 25th and 26th
Information	Tel.: 902 076 621. www.rutadelmodernisme.com
Further details	Timetables may vary. Check updates and information on Route discount at **www.rutadelmodernisme.com** or call 902 076 621

Hospital de Sant Pau - Main entrance

Work started in 1902 and finished around 1926, when the Hospital was finally moved from its old Gothic location in the Raval to the new building.

Domènech i Montaner's work is considered to be one of the best Art Nouveau complexes in the world. The hospital is like a self-contained town, with streets, buildings and gardens. The access pavilion, crowned by a slender clock tower, has the exposed brickwork that predominates in the whole ensemble, with mosaics depicting historical subjects and stone capitals and corbels in the form of angels, sculpted by a young Pau Gargallo. Inside, the main features are the stained glass by Mario Maragliano, the large staircase and the ceilings, which are reminiscent of Islamic architecture. Two dates (1905 with the Greek letter alpha and 1910 with the Greek letter omega) indicate the start and finish of the work on this main building of the complex. The entrance pavilion and the 10 pavilions located around it were built under the personal direction of Domènech i Montaner and show the highly intelligent use of stone, iron and ceramics which is characteristic of the architect. Most of the remaining pavilions, including the huge Casa de Convalescència (Convalescence House), are a later work of Pere Domènech i Roura, the architect's son. Some pavilions were given the names of male or female saints and others the names of Virgins. The pavilions are set among gardens and connected through a network of underground service passages more than one kilometre long. Thus Domènech designed a totally innovative hospital, breaking the building up into a series of cells surrounded by gardens, with a great deal of sunlight and fresh air, in which the patients and doctors enjoyed a far more pleasant natural environment than that of the old medieval hospital. One of the pavilions, currently used as a café, has an unusual Baroque façade, the original front of the old church of Santa Marta designed by Carles Grau in 1735, salvaged and moved to this location when the church was torn down to build the Via Laietana in 1909.

Hospital de Sant Pau - Saint Salvador's pavilion

The hospital occupies 14.5 hectares, the equivalent of nine blocks of the Eixample, and has been restored several times. In 1978 the Modernista pavilions of the hospital were declared a historic artistic monument, and in 1997 the ensemble was listed as UNESCO World Heritage. In the twentieth Century, the Hospital de la Santa Creu i Sant Pau has begun to build a new, larger and more modern building on an adjacent site. This new hospital, however, must respect the harmony of the Modernista pavilions, and only two of the four levels of the new building will be visible, yet surrounded by a small wooded area: the other two will be below ground level. When the new premises come into operation, the Modernista pavilions will be devoted to research, education and cultural activities.

Hospital de Sant Pau
Saint Apollonia's pavilion

Lluís Domènech i Montaner (1849-1923)

The son of a bookbinder, Lluís Domènech i Montaner was born in Barcelona on 27 December 1849. He was a versatile man who combined his passion for drawing with literature, history, deluxe editions, teaching, politics -and of course architecture. Domènech understood the work of an architect as similar to that of an orchestra conductor. He held the baton and all the instruments (the glaziers, the sculptors, the carpenters, the manufacturers of mosaics and paving...) had to sound perfect.

The young Domènech was a brilliant student of physical and natural sciences in Barcelona, and later of engineering in Madrid. This discipline led him finally to study architecture, in which he qualified in 1873. He was a lecturer at the School of Architecture of Barcelona from its foundation in 1875 (so he taught Gaudí and Puig i Cadafalch), and he was director of the School from 1900 to 1920. The publication in 1879 in the journal *La Renaixença* of the article "En busca de una arquitectura nacional" ("The quest for a national architecture") gave him, along with other later works, a certain fame as an art theoretician and disseminator of the latest ideas in architecture, especially those of his much admired Viollet-le-Duc.

Considered today by many to be the "most Modernista" of the artists of Catalan Modernisme, Lluís Domènech did indeed travel and he knew what was being done in the rest of Europe by the artists of the Art Nouveau, Secession and the Arts and Crafts movements, with some of whom he established a friendship. He was, in fact, a humanist of his time, who developed himself in a wide range of fields, including botany, publishing and illustration. He was one of the most outstanding heraldists in the country, a journalist of certain renown and on several occasions he was elected president of the Ateneu Barcelonès, the main cultural association of the time. He had a long political career, starting in a Catalan nationalist movement called Jove Catalunya (Young Catalonia) and reaching the presidency of the Lliga de Catalunya and the Unió Catalanista, the first major parties of the Catalan *Renaixença* (the "Rebirth" of Catalan culture and nationalism, which came to life in the second half of the 19th Century). He was foremost in the drafting of the first declaration of sovereignty for Catalonia, Les Bases de Manresa in 1892, and he was elected member of the Madrid Congress in in 1904 in the so-called "four presidents' ticket", considered to be the first political triumph of Catalan nationalism. Soon, however, Domènech came into conflict with the almighty leader of the Lliga Regionalista, Francesc Cambó, and he abandoned conservative Catalan nationalism to found a new left-wing party, Esquerra Catalana, and to become the editor of its newspaper *El Poble Català*.

The coup d'état by general Primo de Rivera in 1923 led to the dismantling of the regional structures of government in Catalonia, the prohibition of Catalan nationalist political activity at all levels, and the suppression of all but the most naive expressions of Catalan culture (even the Barcelona Football Club stadium was closed!). Domènech, always a passionate lover of life and refinement and of the most civilised forms of expression, felt profoundly affected by the brutal repression of a military regime that he could only see as illegitimate and barbaric. He retired to family life and died that winter, on the same day on which he had been born.

In addition to Barcelona, Domènech performed several important works in Canet de Mar, the home town of the family of his mother, Maria Montaner, and in Reus, thanks to his great friendship with the intellectual Pau Font de Rubinat. (See page 195)

The route now continues by bus. Line 92 (which stops near the intersection of Carrer Sant Antoni M. Claret and Carrer Cartagena, by the main entrance of the Hospital) will take you to **PARK GÜELL**, Gaudí's unfinished urbanistic dream, listed UNESCO World Heritage in 1984. The most ambitious urban planning operation of Barcelona in the late 19th century was idea of Gaudí's main patron, Eusebi Güell, who in 1899 bought an old rural estate of 15 hectares called Can Muntaner de Dalt for conversion into a luxury garden city inspired in Ebenezer Howard's model (and so the name was -and still is- spelt the English way: "Park", as opposed to "Parc", in Catalan). 83 ☆

Predictably, the person entrusted with carrying out Güell's landscape planning scheme was Antoni Gaudí. Gaudí's project involved the construction of a housing estate of 60 private plots and large common greens. Gaudí devised the idea of a bucolic retreat for the highest bourgeoisie of Barcelona. Its location on the hillside and far from the city was ideal to symbolise the metaphor of the ascent to paradise, to Eden. The project, however, was a total failure. Development of the estate began

Park Güell

Address	Olot, s/n; ctra. del Carmel, s/n
Park opens	November through February from 10am to 6pm. March and October, 10am to 7pm. April and September 10am to 8pm. May through August 10am to 9pm
Information	Tel.: 010. www.bcn.es/parcsijardins
Interpretation Centre	Daily 11am to 3pm.
Information	www.museuhistoria.bcn.es or call tel.: 932 856 899
Further details	Timetables may vary. Check updates and information on Route discount at **www.rutadelmodernisme.com** or call 902 076 621

between 1900 and 1904 and was definitively halted in 1914. One plot was purchased by the owner of the construction company developing the works, and two more plots were sold to a single purchaser, who had only one villa built. As for the common facilities, three crosses were built to mark the place where the chapel was to be erected, but only the two entrance pavilions, the retaining walls and all the road infrastructure around a large square supported by columns were completed. As a result of this financial disaster, the heirs of Eusebi Güell, who died in 1918, sold the site to the City Council, and it was decided to preserve it as a public park. The prodigious structures raised among the typical Mediterranean vegetation are a curious mixture of fantasy and spirituality, which the staunch patriot Gaudí interspersed with Catalan emblems. A work, in short, where Gaudí gave up his habitual historicism and boldly chose a language of his own ranging from naturally-inspired forms to a surprisingly avant-garde plasticity.

The main gate of Park Güell, featuring a brick wall decorated with mosaics, is protected by a wrought iron railing and flanked by two evocative pavilions that reproduce the story of Hansel and Gretel, which was performed as an opera at the Liceu in late 1900, the same period Gaudí began to design the Park Güell. The smaller one on the left with a double cross on the roof, is the house of the children Hansel and Gretel: it currently has a bookshop and souvenir shop on the ground floor. The house on the right, crowned by a poisonous toadstool-shaped dome, represents the Witch's dwelling -interestingly, it was meant to be the house of the Park's guard. It now houses the Interpretation Centre of the Park, part of the Barcelona History Museum (open

Park Güell - Main staircase

daily from 11 a.m. to 3 p.m., tel. 932 856 899). The free-access ground floor has information on Gaudí's work, but you must pay a fee to go upstairs to see the original house of the guard and the exhibition "Gaudí and Park Güell. Architecture and Nature". Beyond the two pavilions, on the right one can see a kind of grotto supported by a central column that becomes wider at the top, as if it were a wine glass, meant as a shelter for carriages and horses on rainy days.

The main staircase is parted by a small waterfall featuring the famous multi-coloured dragon of glazed ceramic *trencadís*. The stairs lead to the hypostyle hall, also known as the Hall of the 100 Columns though it only has 86. This hall, originally intended to be the market of the future housing estate, was decorated by Gaudí's assistant Josep Maria Jujol, who was given carte blanche to do so. The result was exceptional: an undulating ceiling of mosaic with varied incrustations forming capricious spirals. When this zone was restored in 1992 lights were added at the base of the columns, which create a spectacular resemblance to a Greek church at night. From the hypostyle hall two paths lead to the great circular square, a marvellous belvedere overlooking the city. According to Gaudí's

Park Güell

Park Güell - Hypostyle Hall

initial design, this square was to collect rainwater, channelled down inside the columns of the hypostyle hall to be collected in a huge cistern holding up to 12,000 cubic metres (not open to the public).

The square is surrounded by a winding bench of *trencadís* in which the imagination of Gaudí and Jujol achieved an extraordinary boldness, considered by some specialists a forerunner of abstract art. The bench is a symphony of colours: greens, blues and yellows are used in different combinations, forming moon shapes and stars and abstract flowers. Colour, however, fades away gradually from left to right, and at the far right the bench is mainly white, the symbol of purity. The bench seems to hint that human life is a kaleidoscope of colours that culminate after death in heavenly white. The white of this part of the bench is not, however, a pure white: here Gaudí used materials that had been

Park Güell - trencadís bench

Park Güell

rejected in other buildings, such as Casa Batlló, precisely because of the "impurity" of this white. The last restoration of the bench (1995) has maintained this imperfection by using up to 21 different hues and shades of white to replace the deteriorated parts.

Other unusual features of the Park Güell are its bridges and viaducts, with twisted, grotto-like columns. The fourth portico that connects the upper part with the lower part is perhaps the most Surrealist structure, with the leaning walls and arches that recall images by Dalí. The summit of the park is crowned by a monumental Calvary formed by three crosses at the place where Gaudí had planned to build the chapel. Even here the feverish architect had symbolic fantasies. If we look toward the east - toward Jerusalem, as it were- the perspective seems to merge all three crosses into one. This is the final point of the ascent: the cross is the ultimate symbol.

The **CASA-MUSEU GAUDÍ** (GAUDÍ MUSEUM-HOUSE) is also within the boundaries of the 84
park. The museum occupies the house in which Antoni Gaudí spent the last 20 years of his life and exhibits interesting elements on the life and work of the brilliant architect. Among other things, visitors can see furniture from Palau Güell **(8)**, the Casa Calvet **(27)** and the Casa Batlló **(45)**, personal objects and souvenirs of Gaudí, in addition to materials and elements of his personal work that provide a particular view of his complex and often vague personality. The house was built under the direction of Francesc Berenguer i Mestres, although the project was signed by Gaudí. The One-day route recommended by the Barcelona Modernisme Route ends here at Park Güell.

Casa-Museu Gaudí

Address	Park Güell; ctra. del Carmel, s/n
Open	Closed on January 1st. December 25th and 26th, and January 6th, open from 10am to 2pm. October through March, 10am to 6pm; April to September, 10am to 8pm
Information	Tel.: 932 193 811.
Further details	Timetables may vary. Check updates and information on Route discount at **www.rutadelmodernisme.com** or call 902 076 621

Casa-Museu Gaudí
Furniture designed by A. Gaudí

To visit the next four houses, you can walk or take number 92 bus at the same stop where you got off for Park Güell. To see Casa Queralt and Finca San Salvador, you get off the bus at the stop called "Passeig de la Mare de Déu del Coll-Funoses Llussà". The same bus takes you to Casa Comas d'Argemir, a few stops onward at "Avinguda República Argentina-Baixada Blanes", and to Cases Ramos, again further on at the stop "Avinguda Príncep d'Astúries, 59".

At the foot of Park Güell one can see the sprawling neighbourhood of Vallcarca, a zone of fervent urban chaos that conceals some small jewels of Modernisme. In Passeig de la Mare de Déu del Coll, near the Creueta del Coll Park (going up Carrer Funoses Llussà and Carrer Pineda), you will find **CASA QUERALT** (Pineda, 12), a curious building by Josep Maria Jujol (1917). Very nearby, going a few metres down the Passeig, is another 85

Casa Queralt

work by Jujol, a student of Gaudí, **FINCA SAN SALVADOR** (SAN SALVADOR ESTATE) (Passeig de la Mare de Déu del Coll, 79 / Pineda, 9), built by Jujol in 1909 and used for years as the bottling plant of Font Radial, a natural spring discovered by chance when work was done on the hill. Jujol never actually finished this project, but he did complete a garden of small terraces adapted to the steep terrain and a series of artificial grottoes to reach the water source. The Barcelona Urban Landscape Institute began to draft a restoration and rehabilitation project for this peculiar place in 2004. 86

Finca San Salvador

From this point you can continue down the Passeig (walking or on bus 92) and

87 following the Viaduct of Vallcarca you will come to **CASA COMAS D'ARGEMIR** (Avinguda de la República Argentina, 92) a work designed by Josep Vilaseca i Casanovas in 1904 that is worthy of attention. From the street one can see its façade in the form of a semi-ellipse, topped with a wrought iron railing with the initials of the owners' names, and decorated with ceramics and discreet sgraffito work around the windows, decorated with lion heads, and the turret, crowned with a pointed dome adorned with blue trencadís.

Casa Comas d'Argemir

88

Down República Argentina (walking or on bus 92) you will reach Plaça Lesseps, where you will find a spectacular yellow Modernista building decorated with floral motifs. The **CASES RAMOS** (Plaça de Lesseps, 30, 31 and 32) are three buildings joined by a common façade built in 1906 by Jaume Torres i Grau. Do not miss the bee-shaped wrought iron banisters of the central balcony. The rear court, at the corner of Carrer Mont-Roig, still has a charming Modernista kiosk. Cinema fans should not miss this building: part of the film *All About my Mother*, by Pedro Almodóvar, was filmed here.

Cases Ramos

☆ 89 Another short downhill walk (or again bus 92) will take us to **CASA VICENS** (Carolines, 18-24). This early work by Gaudí, built between 1883 and 1888, was a commission by Manuel Vicens, a Valencian tile manufacturer, to build a private house in the old municipality of Gràcia. The work had to fulfil two purposes: be the home of the Vicenses and advertise the excellent product that they manufactured. Gaudí gave this house characteristic forms, inspired by Indian and Japanese architecture, and covered a large part of the three façades with spectacular green and white glazed tiles. Gaudí used tiles in this building by exhibiting them in stark contrast to exposed brickwork. Another element of interest on the outside is the iron railing, which reproduces the attractive leaves of *margalló*,

Casa Vicens - General view, an detail of the façade

Casa Vicens - Detail of the railing

the endogenous Catalan palm species (*Chamaerops humilis*). Although the owners may be lenient with discreet visitors who take a step or two into the garden, the house is private property and the interior cannot be visited. Main features of the interior are a spectacular round smoking room, culminated with a Mudejar vault of multi-coloured plaster, elaborate floral decorations and carpentry in the living-room and, generally, the extravagant decoration in the purest style of a Caliph's private chambers.

In the district of Sarrià-Sant Gervasi we find the neighbourhood of Pedralbes, the rich area par excellence of present-day Barcelona. This trend was begun by the Güell family when they decided to develop the land of their estate next to the Gothic Monastery of Pedralbes. Our walk through the district begins at the **PAVELLONS GÜELL** (GÜELL PAVILIONS), of the old Güell Estate. Gaudí dedicated his life to his original vision of architecture and Eusebi Güell gave him the first means to make 90 ☆

Pavellons Güell - Centre del Modernisme

Address	Avinguda de Pedralbes, 15.
Open	Open only for guided visits, Friday through Monday at 10.15am, 11.15am, 12.15am and 1.15pm. Closed on January 1st and 6th, and December 25th and 26th
Information	Tel.: 902 076 621. **www.rutadelmodernisme.com**
Further details	Timetables may vary. Check updates and information on Route discount at **www.rutadelmodernisme.com** or call 902 076 621

Pavellons Güell - Main entrance

such an eccentric type of architecture into a reality. In 1883 Güell wanted to extend the estate that his father had bought and Gaudí was commissioned to carry out parts of this project, under the direction of Joan Martorell. Gaudí designed the gatehouses and garden of the entrance to the estate from the old Sarrià road. In the late 19th century, the estate was mainly used as summer residence by the Güells, though its crops still provided some profit.

Pavellons Güell - Details of the pavilions

For this job, Gaudí took inspiration from the Garden of the Hesperides as depicted by Jacint Verdaguer in his great epic poem *L'Atlàntida.* Verdaguer had dedicated this work -a sort of Catalan remake of Greek myths- to Güell's father-in-law, the Marquis of Comillas, and had in fact finished writing the book on a stay in this very estate. The entrance features the striking Dragon Gate, a five-metre wrought iron sculpture that symbolises the mythological dragon of Verdaguer, with bat's wings, a scaly body, great fangs and a sinuous tongue. The beast is not challenging Saint George here, but Hercules, as Verdaguer blended Catalan symbols with the classic references to produce his own images. The legendary tree in the Garden of Hesperides from which Hercules had to steal a golden apple, for instance, was in Verdaguer's poem an orange tree, considered somewhat more Mediterranean. Crowning the right jamb of the gate, Gaudí placed a small sculpture of an orange tree, with little golden oranges. After the death of Eusebi Güell in 1918, the estate fell into disuse and the heirs granted part of the land for the construction of the Palau Reial de Pedralbes, the Spanish Royal Family's official residence in Barelona. The gate, the old stables and gatekeeper's house have been preserved and are now property of the University of Barcelona: the research centre Càtedra Gaudí has its offices here.

Pavellons Güell - The Dragon Gate

Crossing Avinguda de Pedralbes is Passeig Manuel Girona, and a short walk away is another work by Gaudí, the **PORTAL MIRALLES** of the Miralles Estate (Passeig de Manuel Girona, 55-61). Gaudí's intervention (1901-1902) was limited to the undulating wall and the huge entrance gate to the estate with its peculiar metal-frame eaves. 91

Portal Miralles

If you walk along Passeig Manuel Girona and Ronda del General Mitre you will come to

☆ 92 Carrer Ganduxer, now in the neighbourhood of Sarrià. On this street is the **COL·LEGI DE LES TERESIANES** (THERESIAN SCHOOL Ganduxer, 85-105) which is not open to the public although on occasions, out of school hours, it is allowed to enter the garden and see it.

Col·legi de les Teresianes

Address	Ganduxer, 85-105
Further details	The nuns themselves sometimes organize guided visits to the school: ask the guard at the door or call 932 123 354

In 1888 Gaudí was commissioned to build this spiritual fortress of Saint Theresa. To carry out the commission, Gaudí read the mystical works of the Catholic saint, and it shows. The symbolism of Saint Theresa is everywhere, as in the T-shaped columns at the end of the cloister corridor. In the centre of the 'fortress' there is another column, but it is very simple, because Gaudí imagined that the centre was God's place and he considered that he could not pretend to create anything to match such absolute beauty. The entrance door is also full of religious details, such as the initials of Jesus, although there are also patriotic references in the wrought-iron four-striped Catalan flag. The characteristic Gothic arches of the building represent the

Col·legi de les Teresianes - Central façade

Col·legi de les Teresianes
Roof battlements with the birretas back in place

Col·legi de les Teresianes - Main gate, and interior corridor

symbol of prayer: the parabolic arches on the façades of the building (windows and ornamental motifs) are continued inside. In the corridors of the first floor, the rhythmic presence of these arches generates an interplay of light and shade that enhances the space giving it the feeling of a convent cloister. Gaudí even designed the plant pots, which had to be orange and green in colour. Orange as the symbol of the Holy Trinity, in which yellow is the Father, red the Son and orange, the mixture, is the Holy Spirit. At the corners of the building Gaudí built helicoidal brick pillars with the coat of arms of the Theresian religious order in ceramic, crowned with four-armed crosses. Another interesting element is the chimney, similar to those in Palau Güell, that presides over the roof terrace of the building. In 2002 the Barcelona Urban Landscape Institute recovered elements and emblems of the façade, and replaced the peculiar "birretas" which had disappeared during the Spanish Civil War -University doctoral caps, yat another sybol of Saint Theresa- back on the roof battlements.

Up Carrer Ganduxer you will come to Passeig de la Bonanova. If you turn left, near to the convergence of two major roads you will find the **CASA MULEY-AFID** (Passeig de la Bonanova, 55), a work by Josep Puig i Cadafalch, built in 1911 as a commission for a Moroccan sultan exiled in Barcelona who became very popular because he donated an elephant cow, known as Julia, to the Barcelona Zoo. The building has a certain oriental flavour and is one of the few old mansions in La Bonanova that has not fallen victim to urban development. The building is presently the Mexican Consulate and has been completely restored. 93

Casa Muley-Afid

Not far away, going towards Plaça Sarrià, down Carrer Major de Sarrià and taking Carrer Pedró de la Creu and Carrer del Trinquet, is another work by Puig i Cadafalch: **CASA SASTRE I MARQUÉS** (SASTRE I MARQUÉS HOUSE. Eduardo Conde, 44), a house dating from 1905 in which the

94

Casa Sastre i Marqués

architect combined exposed brickwork with sgraffito work and glazed tiles. From this point, go up Carrer del Trinquet, turn right into Carrer dels Caponata and continue to Carrer del Cardenal Sentmenat, where you take the FGC (S1 or S2 lines) at Sarrià Station to Peu del Funicular Station (at this stop the first wagon does not open its doors, so remember to get on at one of the back wagons!).

Vallvidrera is one of the most singular areas in Barcelona because of its privileged geographic location overlooking the city from the heights. This former town, independent from Barcelona until 1890 and part of the Sarrià-Sant Gervasi district today, still preserves some of its essential character: pure air, enviable landscapes and beautiful Modernista buildings. The quickest way to get here from the city centre is by the FGC underground.

The **CONJUNT FUNICULAR DE VALLVIDRERA** (FUNICULAR RAILWAY OF VALLVIDRERA. Lower station, Avinguda de Vallvidrera, 66, upper station, Queralt, 20), which opened in 1906, has two Modernista buildings by Bonaventura Conill i Montobbio: the **ESTACIÓ INFERIOR** (LOWER STATION), which has suffered major alterations, and the **ESTACIÓ SUPERIOR DE VALLVIDRERA** (VALLVIDRERA UPPER STATION), whose best feature is the façade, featuring windows and a door with voluptuous curved lines. 95

Funicular de Vallvidrera - Estació superior

From the lower station, go down Avinguda de Vallvidrera, and you will see the **CASA MANUEL DOLCET** (MANUEL DOLCET HOUSE. Avinguda de Vallvidrera, 44 interior), a 1907 Modernista building by Joan Rubió i Bellvé featuring a side tower and an open terrace crowned by four Solomonic columns. 96

Casa Manuel Dolcet

Continue down to the end of Avinguda de Vallvidrera, cross Carrer del General Vives and take the number 60 bus (General Vives-Isaac Albèniz stop), to the third stop (Ronda de Dalt-Bellesguard), and then walk along Carrer del General Vives, Carrer Terré and Carrer
97 Benedetti. On the way you will go past the **CASA ALEMANY** (ALEMANY HOUSE. General Vives, 29), another building by Joan Rubió i Bellvé dating from 1901 and built in brick and stone

Casa Alemany

with elements of Arabian inspiration. Now go down Carrer de Bellesguard to the **TORRE BELLESGUARD** (BELLESGUARD VILLA. Bellesguard, 20). This mansion, which Gaudí designed for Maria Sagués in 1900, was finished in 1902. These two years are considered to mark the dividing line between the architect's early and mature work. Gaudí was able to integrate the building perfectly into its natural setting and landscape, whilst respecting its historical content. The medieval ruins of the summer residence of King Martin 1st, the last monarch of the Barcelona dynasty (15th century), were used as a starting point for designing the new building whilst dignifying the historical remains. Gaudí built it to resemble a Gothic-style medieval castle in: the façade is clad in a slate-type stone of grey and green hues, decorated with square boss-type elements and dotted with a large number of windows and with trefoil arches. More than a century after its construction, the building is still a private residence. 98 ☆

Torre Bellesguard

Nearby one can see the arches that Gaudí himself designed between 1903 and 1905 in order to consolidate the street leading to Sant Gervasi cemetery and passing next to the Torre Bellesguard. The ten arches are little known, although they are contemporary, and very similar, to the famous arches the architect designed for the Park Güell.

From here go along Carrer de Bellesguard, Carrer de Quatre Camins and Carrer de Císter, where you will come to a **TORRE UNIFAMILIAR** (SINGLE-FAMILY VILLA. Melilla, 9, Císter, 25) built by an unknown architect in 1907, whose most emblematic feature is a belvedere tower on the 99 corner. It currently houses a café-restaurant. Turn right into Carrer de Melilla and go down

100 Carrer dels Dominics to the **CASA RIALP** (RIALP HOUSE. Dominics, 14) by Joan Rubió i Bellvé, dating from 1908, with interesting exposed brickwork and rubble walls. In the interior, which is not open to visitors, there are paintings by Joaquim Torres García, an Uruguayan painter who lived in Barcelona at the time. Continue along Carrer dels Dominics, Carrer de Vendrell, Carrer del Císter and Passeig de Sant Gervasi to Plaça de John Kennedy, at the bottom of Avinguda del Tibidabo, another neighbourhood of Barcelona where many Modernista works are to be found.

To reach the Tibidabo area from any other part of the city you can take Line 7 of the FGC underground to Avinguda del Tibidabo station, or bus numbers 17, 22, 58, 73, 75 and 123, which take you to the bottom of the avenue.

Casa Rialp

Avinguda del Tibidabo, which begins at the crossroads of Passeig de Sant Gervasi and Carrer Balmes, is a living memory of the early 20th century Barcelona bourgeoisie. In 1889, the entrepreneur and chemist Salvador Andreu -who made pots of money with his famous pills for sore throats- set out to build an amusement park on the hill overlooking Barcelona. To develop this somewhat eccentric dream, Andreu established the company El Tibidabo, with which he bought the large area of

La Rotonda

barren land stretching from the hilltop down towards the sea to Passeig Sant Gervasi. On these slopes he created a garden city along an elegant avenue, which he opened in 1901 when already a few splendid private residences were being built. The Tibidabo Modernisme walk begins at **LA ROTONDA** (Avinguda del Tibidabo, 2), an interesting 101
Modernista building built by Adolf Ruiz i Casamitjana in 1906 to house a hotel, the Metropolitan. The building is now a clinic.

Near La Rotonda, at the beginning of Avinguda del Tibidabo, there is a stop where you can catch the **TRAMVIA BLAU** (BLUE TRAM). This tram, which originally dates from the 102
Modernista period, is a pleasant way to approach the mountain, on a relaxed ride between majestic houses and gardens up to the funicular lower station. The six trams on the route cover the distance of 1,276 metres, including a difference in altitude of 93 metres, at an average speed of 10 kph. The Tramvia Blau's first service on 29 October 1901 was the fulfilment of Doctor Salvador Andreu's ambition to open up an alternative way to the Tibidabo, direct to his funfair at the summit.

Tramvia Blau

Address	Avinguda del Tibidabo, s/n
Open	Timetables may vary with the seasons, it is advised to chek them beforehand
Information	Tel.: 933 187 074 or tel.: 010. www.tmb.net
Further details	Check updates and information on Route discount at **www.rutadelmodernisme.com** or call 902 076 621

At first the fleet consisted of four trams that covered the route between Passeig de Sant Gervasi, the end of the line for Barcelona's urban trams, and the lower station of the Tibidabo funicular half way up the mountain. In 1981, following a long period of restoration work, two old trams were put back into operation: tram number 2 from 1901, which had been out of service for 30 years, and the model popularly known as "la Jardinera" ("the Flower Box") which had once run along the sea front. The renewal of the tracks on 1984 and the construction work on the city's second ring road in 1990 affected the line's old route. However, advantage was taken of this circumstance to build a new transformer station and refurbish the tracks and the tram sheds.

Tramvia Blau

On the way up Avinguda del Tibidabo you go past three buildings on the opposite side of the road, regarded as belonging to the post-Modernista *Noucentista* movement. Two on the left hand side: **TORRE DEL DOCTOR ANDREU** (DOCTOR ANDREU'S VILLA. Avinguda del Tibidabo, 17-19), and **TORRE SALVADOR ANDREU** (SALVADOR ANDREU'S VILLA. Avinguda del Tibidabo, 21; Josep M. Florensa, 1), both built in the period 1915-1918 by Enric Sagnier i Villavecchia. On the right side, you can see **CASA COLL** (avinguda del Tibidabo, 28), now a private school but originally a residence, also by the prolific Enric Sagnier. Just in front
103 of Casa Coll, again on the left hand side of the road, is the Modernista **TORRE IGNACIO PORTABELLA** (avinguda del Tibidabo, 27; Teodor Roviralta, 4) a remarkable work by the master builder José Pérez Terraza (1905), a two-story villa with a semi-circular belvedere.

Torre Ignacio Portabella

Casa Roviralta - El frare blanc

The next stop on the Route is a building built in phases (1903-1913) by Joan Rubió i Bellvé: **CASA ROVIRALTA** (avinguda del Tibidabo, 31; Romà Macaya, 1-5). Popularly known as "el Frare Blanc" ("the White Friar") from the times when it was the home of the Roviralta family. It is now a restaurant proudly showing off its austere white walls and a roof with large eaves, much in Rubió's style. 104

Further on up the road there is another building by Rubió i Bellvé (1903), **CASA FORNELLS** (avinguda del Tibidabo, 35-37; Bosch i Alsina, 1). It is built in a medievalist style in which the use of exposed brickwork, so characteristic of this architect, predominates. Leaving Avinguda del 105

Casa Fornells

Tibidabo, turn into Bosch i Alsina and keep going until you see **COSMOCAIXA-MUSEU DE LA CIÈNCIA** (COSMOCAIXA-SCIENCE MUSEUM). The museum is partly housed in a Modernista building by Josep Domènech i Estapà, constructed between 1904 and 1909 as a home for the blind. A new building has been attached in 2004 to open CosmoCaixa Barcelona, the new Science Museum of the "la Caixa" Foundation, and Domènech's building is now mainly 106 ☆

Museu de la Ciència - CosmoCaixa

Address	Teodor Roviralta, 47-51
Open	Tuesday to Sunday, from 10am to 8pm. Closed on Mondays (except if holiday) and on January 1st and 6th and December 25th
Information	Tel.: 932 126 050. www.fundacio.lacaixa.es
Further details	Timetables may vary. Check updates and information on Route discount at **www.rutadelmodernisme.com** or call 902 076 621

used for administrative and educational purposes, and for the museum's restaurant.The actual museum is in a modern, spacious building, and has been specially designed to be attractive both to children and adults, with a wide range of scientific and educational information, exhibitions, conferences, workshops, seminars and debates. The permanent exhibit, the Matter Hall, leads the visitor through time, from the Big Bang to present day. The Flooded Forest and the Geological Wall are two of the main features of this exhibit. CosmoCaixa also has a planetarium and several areas specifically for children, and activities are constantly going on in its Auditorium and conference halls. The museum has also opened a new public space to the city, the Plaça de la Ciència (Science Square).

107 From this point, go down Carrer del Císter to the **CONVENT DE VALLDONZELLA** (VALLDONZELLA MONASTERY. Císter, 39-45) by Bernardí Martorell i Puig in 1910. It has a Gothic style with Gaudinian influences.

To get back to Avinguda del Tibidabo, cross over the Ronda, just in front of the Museum, and continue along Carrer Adrià Margarit to
108 see **CASA MUNTADAS** (MUNTADAS HOUSE. Avinguda del Tibidabo, 48), a handsome building by Josep Puig i Cadafalch in 1901 that re-creates the façade of a typical Catalan farmhouse, or *masia*, decorated with simple stucco flower designs framing the doors and windows and following the contours of the
109 crown. A little further up is **CASA CASACUBERTA** (avinguda del Tibidabo, 56), by Joan Rubió i Bellvé (1907), featuring a wide variety of richly decorated doors and windows

Casa Muntadas

Casa Casacuberta

that are one of this architect's trademarks. At the top of Avinguda del Tibidabo, where the Tramvia Blau route terminates, is Plaça del Doctor Andreu, with a music bar at either end of the square. Just in front of the Mirablau bar is one of the area's largest buildings, **CASA EVARIST ARNÚS** 110 (Manuel Arnús, 1-31). Residence of the Arnús bankers family, this estate -also known as "el Pinar" ("the Pine Grove")- was designed by the inevitable Enric Sagnier i Villavecchia in 1903. A little

further on is the estate caretakers' house, which is also in Neo-Gothic style. This mansion provides one of the typical night sites of this district: when floodlit, it appears like a castle out of a fairy tale.

From Plaça del Doctor Andreu you can take the funicular up to the top of the Tibidabo and
111 the **PARC D'ATRACCIONS TIBIDABO** (TIBIDABO FUNFAIR). The Tibidabo Funfair of Barcelona, opened in 1899 by doctor Salvador Andreu, is one of the three oldest in the world. Its magnificent location, in a natural environment where engineering gems of great historical value -the so-called "emblematic rides"- are found side-by-side with state-of-the-art installations and startling shows, make this one of the most representative leisure spots in Barcelona.

Parc d'Atraccions Tibidabo

Address	Plaça del Tibidabo, 3-4
Open	Timetables vary with the seasons, it is advised to check them beforehand
Information	Tel.: 932 117 942. www.tibidabo.es
Getting there	"Tibibus", direct from Plaça Catalunya; or FGC metro, stopping at Peu del Funicular, then take Funicular de Vallvidrera or BUS 111 to the mountain top
Further details	Check updates and information on Route discount at **www.rutadelmodernisme.com** or call 902 076 621

The emblematic fairground attractions include the Avió (Aeroplane), which is part of the city's collective memory, and the Museu d'Autòmats (Automaton Museum), housed in a former theatre dating from 1909. The automaton collection includes pieces from all over the world and some fifty automatons from the early 20th century, some of which are

considered to be Modernista. Many of them still work; they range from coin-operated dolls that were once a common sight at fairs throughout Europe, to mechanical games and toys with which the children of the bourgeoisie of the time used to amuse themselves. The museum's collection is regarded as one of the best in the world, particularly because of the good condition of many of the items, some of which are currently being restored.

Parc d'Atraccions Tibidabo
Machine in the Automaton Museum, and general view

From the fairground you can walk down Carretera de Vallvidrera al Tibidabo, where you will find a turn-off taking you the Fabra Observatory. It is a pleasant stroll, but if you don't want to walk the only way to get here is by taxi or private transport. From Barcelona you take Carretera de Sant Cugat (formerly known as Arrabassada) to Carretera de Vallvidrera al Tibidabo. The **OBSERVATORI FABRA** (FABRA OBSERVATORY) 112 ☆ belongs to the Barcelona Royal Academy of Arts and Sciences, which is in charge of its operation and maintenance. Opened in 1904, the building was designed by the Barcelonan architect Josep Domènech i Estapà. The origin of the Fabra Observatory goes back to the year 1900, when Camil Fabra, the philanthropic industrialist who

Observatori Fabra

Address	Carretera de l'Observatori Fabra, s/n
Open	All year round: schedules follow the astronomical calendar
Information	Tel.: 902 502 220.
Getting there	From the mountain top, it is a nice stroll down Cafrretera de Vallvidrera al Tibidabo. From Barcelona, you need a taxi or private transport: follow Carretera de Sant Cugat and turn at Carretera de Vallvidrera al Tibidabo.
Further details	Check updates and information on Route discount at **www.rutadelmodernisme.com** or call 902 076 621

Observatori Fabra

became first Marquis of Alella, donated a handsome legacy for the construction of an astronomical, meteorological and seismic observatory on Tibidabo. Construction began in 1902 and was completed two years later in 1904.

The building, formed by the juxtaposition of three clearly differentiated bodies (one octagonal, one rectangular and the other in the shape of a cross), is the result of the typical eclectic approach of Domènech i Estapà in dealing with the special purposes for which it was intended. The rectangular volume, ending in a crossing, is cut in two by the vertical opening required for the operation of research equipment, and the octagonal body is crowned by a rotating metal dome, housing the telescope. On the seaward side, the building is decorated by a classically inspired porch which boasts two Neo-Egyptian columns and a pediment with very unusual shapes. The pediment also features a bas-relief depicting the figure of a half-naked woman holding an astrolabe in her left hand. The figure is surrounded by representations of planets and stars, among which you can recognise the Sun and Saturn, so it may be said to be an allegory of astronomy.

Astronomical activity began in 1905 with the observation of an eclipse and has never stopped since, although the most relevant scientific contribution to astronomy were Josep Comas i Solà's observations and discoveries between 1915 and 1930. Research is still carried out at the Fabra Observatory, but a space has been opened for educational activities and to popularise astronomy among the general public. A new project aimed at schools has started as well as a cycle of night-time observations entitled "Barcelona's Sky" intended to show visitors the heavenly bodies that can be seen from the city. An interesting option are the "Suppers under the Stars", in which the visit includes dinner at the garden, a visit to the observatory and the chance to have a glimpse at the stars through its great century-old telescope (only in July, August and September; it is required to book in advance).

The district of Sant Andreu has a very distinct personality as a result of its long tradition of manufacturing industries and grassroots cultural activities. Three important pieces of its Modernista past have been preserved. On a corner of Gran de Sant Andreu is the modest **CASA VIDAL** (Pons i Gallarza, 1-3 / Gran de Sant Andreu, 255), an apartment building with a pale green façade built in 1906 by the local architect Joan Torras i Guardiola. Interesting features are the wrought iron balcony railings, with sinuous forms that enhance 113

Casa Vidal

the unusual roundness of this corner. To the right, on number 306 of this street you will find Farmàcia Guinart, an unusual 1896 chemists'. To the left, continuing along Carrer Gran de Sant Andreu you will come to Passeig Fabra i Puig, the former Rambla de Sant Andreu, where on the corner of Carrer Cuba stands **CAN GUARDIOLA** (Passeig Fabra i Puig, 13 / Cuba, 2-4), a small Modernista jewel built by Josep Codina i Clapés in 1904. The main interest here is in the decorative features: the crown of the main façade, which is reminiscent of Catalan Baroque, or the balcony doors, which seem to be inspired in the scarce Barcelonan Plateresque. Turning back, cross the Passeig and continue along Carrer Monges. At the intersection of this street and Carrer Vallès stands the small **ESGLÉSIA DE SANT PACIÀ**. The interest of this modest parish church built in 1895 lies in its interior, where you can see a mosaic, the **MOSAÏC DE L'ESGLÉSIA DE SANT PACIÀ** (Vallès, 40) that Antoni Gaudí designed in his first years as an architect. 114 115

Can Guardiola

Mosaic de l'Església de Sant Pacià

Forever beautiful

Some of the oldest commercial establishments of Barcelona boast a plate, set in the pavement in front of the entrance, with an inscription in which the Council acknowledges their long-lasting contribution to the city's heritage. The plate is made of cast iron, with designs allegoric of different commercial activities and the year in which the shop opened. This is the *Guapos per sempre* (Forever Beautiful) plate, awarded by the Barcelona Urban Landscape Institute since 1993 to distinguish some old shops -and generations of shopkeepers- that have kept business afloat into a modern economy and yet managed to preserve the distinct character and the original artistic values of the establishment. Award winners all have more than half a century of continued activity within the original commercial sector and in the same neighbourhood and, most importantly, have all made an effort to preserve their original outer appearance. In 2004 up to 105 establishments had a *Guapos per sempre* plate on their doorstep: here is a selection of the Modernista awards.

15 ANTIGA CASA FIGUERAS - PASTISSERIA ESCRIBÀ

La Rambla. 83 - Petxina, 1

In 1902 Jaume Figueras commissioned Antoni Ros, a painter and scenic artist, to decorate his shop, which manufactured and sold pasta. A whole team of artists worked with Ros, including the sculptor Lambert Escaler, the glaziers Rigalt & Granell and Mario Maragliano for the mosaics. The façade is a magnificent example of the integration of the different decorative arts, with its diversity of volumes and finishes: stone, symbolist sculptural relief, mosaics, leaded windows and wrought-iron. In 1986 the shop was taken over and restored by the reputed Escribà bakers.

11 CAFÈ DE L'ÒPERA

La Rambla, 74

Though the current café dates from 1929, it had been previously founded as Xocolateria La Mallorquina in around 1890. The main door has a wooden frame with carved natural motifs, combined with two marble door jambs. The interior is in pre-Modernista (*Vuitcentista*) style with use of cast-iron columns, painted cloth panels and mirrors with etched designs representing female figures from several operas.

10 CAMISERIA BONET

La Rambla, 72

This outfitter's was founded in 1890 and was managed until late 2002 by three generations of the Bonet family. On the façade a complete wooden cladding rises to the mezzanine, a space originally occupied by the workshop, with a display cabinet framed by two signs made of hammered sheet metal. The wood used throughout the shop is mahogany, with small floral decorations in the corners. In July 2002 Camiseria Bonet won the Commercial Tradition Prize awarded by the Generalitat (government) of Catalonia. It recently changed ownership.

CASA TEIXIDOR

Rda. Sant Pere, 16

In 1909 the architect Manuel Joaquim Raspall carried out the design of this shop with the collaboration of artists such as Lluís Bru -who signed his mosaic decoration under the shop sign- and the Buixeras glaziers. The iron work adopts natural forms and provides the framework for the design, both in the upper part and at the side of the doors, and the result is a clear example of integration of the arts. The interior recalls the original business, a fine art supplies shop with painted signs indicating sections on architecture, painting and drawing. The premises are now used by an optician's.

CONFITERIA J. REÑÉ

Consell de Cent, 362

This establishment was opened in 1910 as a cake shop, although in 1892 the Reñé family had already set up their chocolate factory, La Suiza-Reñé, in it.

The shop was redecorated by Enric Llardent using mainly two materials: marble for the skirting of the shop window and Cuban mahogany for all the joinery. In the interior he adapted the large display cabinets, also with wooden joinery, and the plaster decoration of the ceiling. In 2003, the establishment became a café-restaurant.

EL INGENIO

Rauric, 6

Since 1838 when the sculptor Escaler opened El Ingenio, this shop has specialised in items for parties and festivals. Escaler's successors, the Homs-Cardona family, have maintained the traditional business and also preserved the decoration of the shop. At the entrance it has wood panelling featuring gilt wooden mouldings and medallion decorations.

Inside all the walls are lined with original wooden shelves and cabinets of simple design. The rear workshop can be visited on occasions.

23 ELS QUATRE GATS

Montsió, 3 bis

Casa Martí, by Josep Puig i Cadafalch in 1896, houses the bar-restaurant Els Quatre Gats founded by Pere Romeu and Miquel Utrillo, which remained open in this first lapse only until 1903. The interior of the establishment reveals the Neo-Gothic style of the building and the attempt to recreate a characteristically Catalan rural space with the ceramic decoration and floral and geometric forms, the stone frames and the different elements of wrought-iron.

50 FARMÀCIA A. BOLÓS

Rambla Catalunya, 77 - València, 256

Farmàcia Bolós is a chemists' shop situated on the ground floor of a building by Domènech i Estapà. On both the interior and the exterior it still has the original 1902 decoration by Antoni Falguera, according to a design by pharmacist Novelles himself. One of the main features is the main door, with straight lines at the bottom but crowned by a panel of undulating lines and floral motifs. The leaves on the leaded glass door are framed in a rich woodwork, and depict an orange tree together with the name of the former owners. The interior still has the original decoration; display cabinets, stained glass, mural paintings and a collection of pharmaceutical china and pottery containers.

FARMÀCIA CASAUS

Aribau, 91

Formerly Farmàcia Sañé and founded in 1901, this chemists' shop maintains the original decoration on both the façade and the interior. The cladding of the façade has austere, geometric lines. The two entrances are made of wood, with simple garlands as a basic decorative motif, and bevelled glass etched with the same design. In the interior it still has the display cabinets and counter, though they have been adapted to present-day needs.

FARMÀCIA ENRICH

Muntaner, 83

Founded in 1902. At the entrance, iron is the basic element framing the stained glass windows with geometric forms. At the top the main features are the decoration of garlands and undulating lines, in contrast with the dominant straight lines of the central glazed panel, and at the bottom again the undulating iron skirting, characteristic of Modernisme. Important features are the branch-shaped wrought-iron handles and two pharmaceutical motifs etched on the side windows. In the interior the whole wooden display cabinet with floral motifs in the corners has been preserved.

FARMÀCIA FERRER ARGELAGUET

Roger de Llúria, 74

This Modernista style chemists' shop was founded in 1906 as Farmàcia Robert. In the interior, it still keeps all the wooden display cabinets with rich natural motifs, together with the counter and cash desk. Other outstanding features are the ceiling with a *trompe l'oeil* representation of a bandstand, and the plaster mouldings decorated with garlands. The name of the former chemist's shop can be seen etched in the glass of the door.

FARMÀCIA GUINART

Gran de Sant Andreu, 306

Founded in 1896, this chemists' conserves its Modernista elements practically intact. On the façade one can see the wrought-iron work with undulating forms as a decorative motif at the ends and covering the wood on the doors. These are now totally made of wood, though the lower part was originally marble. The yellow and blue ceramic work was manufactured in the Xumetra kilns in this same Sant Andreu district.

FARMÀCIA MADROÑAL

Comte Borrell, 133

On the corner of Gran Via and Carrer Comte Borrell we find two attached apartment buildings, with a chemists' on the ground floor. The Farmàcia Madroñal was first opened in 1901 and still preserves elements from this time, such as the wrought-iron lantern , a typical element used to identify chemists' in those times.

FARMÀCIA NORDBECK

Ausiàs Marc, 31

The design of this chemists' shop is attributed to the architect E. Catà, around 1905. Its outstanding features are the wooden panels with floral decoration on the façade, the wrought-iron work, and the stained glass friezes that crown both window and door. Inside one can still see the original furnishings with a predominance of undulating lines and floral motifs, particularly on the counter.

FARMÀCIA PUIGORIOL

Mallorca, 312 - Girona, 125

This chemists' shop is attributed to Marià Pau, who seems to have decorated it in 1913-14, together with a team of decorators including Francesc Torres, who did the oak woodwork of the frames, Pere Anglès who made the furniture and the Nogués brothers who fitted the marble skirting. Look out for the stones incrusted in the bevelled external glazing. Original objects -the gas lights, the ceramic pots and the furnishings- are still preserved inside.

FILATÈLIA NUMISMÀTICA MONGE

Boters, 2

The current Monge stamp and coin collecting shop replaced the original lingerie shop, Llenceria Jaumà, in the 1940s, but kept the outer appearance intact. It features a decoration with carved wood and symbolic reliefs covering the door jambs, framing the sign with circular forms and covering the lower part of the façade with jointed panels. The original decoration of the shop dates approximately from 1904.

40 FORN SARRET

Girona, 73

This bakery was decorated in around 1898, and is striking because of the overall impression created by the wooden frames, which house the sign with curving lines and oval shapes that extend to the façade of the building. On the wall between the two entrance doors there is a shield showing a woman reaping. The sign is now printed, but could originally have been of leaded glass.

GRILL ROOM

Escudellers, 8

Formerly known as Petit Torino, this bar occupying the ground floor of a previous Vuitcentista building was decorated in Modernista style by Ricard Capmany around 1902. The façade is clad in wood and features a central window crowned by a shield depicting a raging bull, the symbol of the Vermut Torino company. An interesting feature of the doors is the glasswork at the top. In the interior the display cabinet of sinuous lines with natural motifs and the two counters, one completely plain and the other with applied ceramics, have been conserved. Other outstanding features are the cast iron pillars and the painted panelled ceiling in the first section of the premises.

12 HOTEL ESPAÑA

Sant Pau, 9-11

In 1903 the architect Domènech i Montaner was commissioned to decorate the Fonda Espanya, and his work won the City Council prize for the best establishment.

Inside some of the rooms have been conserved intact, with wood and ceramic wainscots with heraldic motifs, mural paintings of marine themes and other ornamental elements. One of the rooms features an alabaster fireplace made in 1901 by the sculptor Eusebi Arnau.

HOTEL REGINA

Bergara, 2-4

The Hotel Regina, founded in 1917, conserves a canopy from the time of its foundation which is a good example of Modernista decorative arts. The structure is of wrought iron with leaded glass decorated with natural themes. It is covered by a frosted glass vault. The polychrome stained glass shows the date of foundation and two initials, FR, belonging to the first owner, Francesc Recasens.

56 QUEVIURES MÚRRIA

Roger de Llúria, 85

This shop was opened under the name "La Puríssima" in 1898 as a coffee roasters', and it is currently a grocer's shop under different ownership. All the exterior decoration has been conserved, the main features being the signs and the glazed advertisements, above all the traditional "Anís del Mono". Slight modifications have been made to the interior but the cash desk has been preserved, as have the counter and the rear cabinets, all in Scotch pine with simple geometrical decoration.

PAVIMENTS ESCOFET

Rda. Universitat, 20

The firm Mosaics Escofet, which specialises in hydraulic floor tiles, was originally located at Ronda de Sant Pere, Nº 8. In 1890, the shop was moved to the actual site, together with all of its original interior and exterior decoration, work of Josep Pascó (1856-1920), mosaicist and teacher at the Llotja art school.

The establishment has a cladding of artificial stone panels decorated with floral motifs and framed in wood. The Modernista motifs are concentrated in the sign and the upper railings, whereas in the rest a paving design by the same decorator is repeated.

19 RESTAURANT VIENA

La Rambla, 115

Viena is a local fast-food bar opened 15 years ago on the premises of the former sausage shop Xarcuteria Mumbrú, founded in 1889, and it still preserves the original decoration. Wood is used throughout to frame glass panels painted with floral motifs: on the wainscot, on the cabinets, on the two cash desks located beside the door as decorative elements and on the bar, which was created using the old counter. Outstanding features are the pictorial decoration and the geometric woodwork on the ceiling.

Actions on Modernista Heritage

City Council Programme *Barcelona, posa't guapa* (*Barcelona, get pretty*)

List of monuments included in the Barcelona Modernisme Route which since 1986 have received technical advice, economic support and other incentives from the Institut Municipal del Paisatge Urbà (Municipal Urban Landscape Institute) for works of restoration and improvement of their architectural heritage.

42 **CASA POMAR** (Girona, 86)

Restoration of façades.

53 **CASA QUERALTÓ** (Rambla de Catalunya, 88)

Restoration of façades.

48 **CASA FARGAS** (Rambla de Catalunya, 47)

Restoration of façades, balconies and carpentry (blinds).

49 **CASA GARRIGA NOGUÉS** (Diputació, 250)

Restoration of façades.

65 **CASA THOMAS** (Mallorca, 293)

Soundproofing.

76 **PALAU DEL BARÓ DE QUADRAS** (Diagonal, 373)

Restoration of façades.

HOTEL REGINA (Bergara, 2-4)

Restoration of façades.

57 **CASA JOSEFA VILLANUEVA** (València, 312)

Restoration of façades, balconies and carpentry (blinds).

26 CASA LLORENÇ CAMPRUBÍ (Casp, 22)

Restoration of façades, carpentry (blinds) and signs.

1 CASA ESTAPÉ (Passeig de Sant Joan, 6)

Restoration of façades.

57 CASA JOSEFA VILLANUEVA (València, 312)

Soundproofing.

47 CASA DOLORS CALM (Rambla de Catalunya, 54)

Landscaping of interior spaces.

60 CONSERVATORI MUNICIPAL DE MÚSICA (Bruc, 104-112)

Restoration of the façade.

98 TORRE BELLESGUARD (Bellesguard, 16-20)

Landscaping of interior spaces.

FARMÀCIA FERRER ARGELAGUET (Roger de Llúria, 74)

Restoration of façades.

44 CASA AMATLLER (Passeig de Gràcia, 41, baixos)

Restoration of the façade and foyer.

51 CASA DOMÈNECH I ESTAPÀ (València, 241)

Restoration of the façade.

70 CASA ANTONI COSTA (Rambla de Catalunya, 122)

Restoration of façades.

79 CASA MACAYA (Passeig de Sant Joan, 108)

Restoration of façades, balconies and carpentry (blinds).

80 CASA PLANELLS (Diagonal, 332)

Restoration of exteriors and recovery of missing volumes.

27 CASA CALVET RESTAURANT CASA CALVET (Casp, 48)

Restoration of façades, balconies and carpentry (blinds).

50 FARMÀCIA BOLÓS (Rambla de Catalunya, 77)

Refurbishment of signs.

113 CASA VIDAL (Pons i Gallarza, 1-3 / Gran de Sant Andreu, 255)

Restoration of the façade. Refurbishment of signs.

FARMÀCIA CASAUS (Aribau, 91)

Restoration of façades.

38 SEU DEL DISTRICTE DE SANTS-MONTJUÏC (Creu Coberta, 106)

Restoration of the façade and stained glass windows of the Plenary Chamber.

23 CASA MARTÍ, ELS QUATRE GATS (Montsió, 3 bis)

Restoration of the façade and the Modernista railing.

55 BANCS - FANALS (Passeig de Gràcia, s/n)

Restoration of the bench-lampposts.

2 HIDROELÈCTRICA (Av. de Vilanova, 12)

Restoration of façades.

11 CAFÈ DE L'ÒPERA (Rambla, 74)

Restoration of façades, balconies and blinds.

56 QUEVIURES MÚRRIA (Roger de Llúria, 85)

Restoration of façades, balconies and carpentry (blinds).

88 CASES RAMOS (Plaça de Lesseps, 30, 31 i 32)

Restoration of façades, balconies and carpentry (blinds) and recovery of pavilion.

61 CASA LAMADRID (Girona, 113)

Restoration of façades, balconies and carpentry (blinds).

CASA PAU UBARRI (València, 293)

Restoration of façades.

112 OBSERVATORI FABRA (Ctra. de l'Observatori, s/n)

Restoration of the façade.

19 REIAL ACADÈMIA DE CIÈNCIES I ARTS (Rambla, 115)

Restoration of the façade and the towers.

27 CASA CALVET (Casp, 48)

Restoration of façades and balconies.

RESTAURANT VIENA (Rambla, 115)

Restoration of façade.

38 **SEU DEL DISTRICTE DE SANTS-MONTJUÏC** (Creu Coberta, 106)

Restoration of the staircase and the Plenary Chamber.

60 **CONSERVATORI MUNICIPAL DE MÚSICA** (Bruc, 104-112)

Restoration of the roof and skylight.

24 **PALAU DE LA MÚSICA CATALANA** (Sant Francesc de Paula, 2)

Restoration of sculpture by Miquel Blay.

62 **CASA GRANELL** (Girona, 122)

Restoration of exterior façades (ground floor and mezzanine).

FARMÀCIA MADROÑAL (Compte Borrell, 133)

Restoration of the exterior façades.

COLMADO CASAS (Pau Claris / Provença)

Reproduction of the Modernista poster by Ramon Casas.

83 **PARK GÜELL** (Olot, s/n)

Restoration of the central staircase.

71 **CASA SAYRACH** (Diagonal, 423)

Restoration of the façade and recovery of the ground floor.

88 **CASES RAMOS** (Plaça de Lesseps, 30, 31 i 32)

Replacement of individual aerials by collective ones and restoration of roof terrace.

40 **FORN SARRET** (Girona, 73)

Restoration of stuccoes and cornices on the façades.

54 **CASA VÍDUA MARFÀ** (Passeig de Gràcia, 66)

Restoration of exterior façades.

87 **CASA COMAS D'ARGEMIR** (Av. de la República Argentina, 92)

Restoration of exterior and interior façades.

15 **ANTIGA CASA FIGUERAS** (Rambla, 83)

Restoration of exterior façades.

52 **CASA JUNCOSA** (Rambla de Catalunya, 78)

Interior façades.

91 **PORTAL MIRALLES** (Passeig de Manuel Girona, 55-61)

Full restoration of lost elements, consolidation of the internal structure, illumination and paving of the surrounding area and erection of a sculpture dedicated to Antoni Gaudí.

PAVIMENTS ESCOFET (Rda. Universitat, 20)

Restoration of exterior façades.

38 **SEU DEL DISTRICTE DE SANTS-MONTJUÏC** (Creu Coberta, 106)

Restoration of interior skylight.

89 **CASA VICENS** (Carolines, 18-24)

Restoration of façade, roof and gallery.

36 **ESTACIÓ DE MAGÒRIA** (Gran Via de les Corts Catalanes, 181-247; Moianès, 1-17)

Restoration of façades.Recovery of the volumetrics of the original building and the roof of the tower, including replacement of the special clock and removal of the added volumes.

26 **CASA LLORENÇ CAMPRUBÍ** (Casp, 22)

Restoration of façades.

61 **CASA LAMADRID** (Girona, 113)

Exterior façades.

63 **CASA LLOPIS BOFILL** (Bailèn, 113)

Restoration of exterior and interior façades, party walls, roof terraces and artistic glasswork. Removal of barriers, replacement of individual aerials by collective ones and substitution of water tanks by connection to network.

7 **FANALS DE GAUDÍ** (Pl. Reial)

Restoration of the lampposts.

23 **CASA MARTÍ, ELS QUATRE GATS** (Montsió, 3 bis)

Restoration of the image of Saint Joseph.

44 **CASA AMATLLER** (Passeig de Gràcia, 41, baixos)

Alterations to the former coach house and the porter's lodge to house the Centre del Modernisme and an exhibition hall.

90 **PAVELLONS GÜELL** (Av. de Pedralbes, 15)

Restoration of the Dragon Gate.

FARMÀCIA ENRICH (Muntaner, 83)

Restoration of exterior façades.

GRILL ROOM (Escudellers, 8)

Restoration of exterior and interior façades and decorated panels on the first floor.

53 **CASA QUERALTÓ** (Rambla de Catalunya, 88)

Restoration of façades.

62 **CASA GRANELL** (Girona, 122)

Replacement of carpentry (blinds).

78 **CASA TERRADES, CASA DE LES PUNXES** (Diagonal, 416-420)

Restoration of façades.

45 **CASA BATLLÓ** (Passeig de Gràcia, 43)

Restoration of exterior façade, roof, inner courtyards and hall.

77 **CASA COMALAT** (Diagonal, 442)

Restoration of exterior façades, artistic glasswork and rear façades and recovery of carpentry (blinds).

CONFITERIA J. REÑÉ (Consell de Cent, 362)

Restoration of façades.

50 **FARMÀCIA BOLÓS** (Rambla de Catalunya, 77)

Restoration of shop.

92 **COL·LEGI DE LES TERESIANES** (Ganduxer, 85-105)

Restoration of various special elements of the crown, coats of arms on the façade and capstones on the battlements.

98 **TORRE BELLESGUARD** (Bellesguard, 16-20)

Restoration of the crown of the building and in particular the outstanding elements: the merlons and gargoyles.

61 **CASA LAMADRID** (Girona, 113)

Thermal and acoustic insulation.

FARMÀCIA ENRICH (Muntaner, 83)

Restoration of the interior façades.

64 **CASA VALLET I XIRÓ** (Mallorca, 302)

Restoration of the exterior façades and thermal and acoustic insulation.

FARMÀCIA MADROÑAL (Compte Borrell, 133)

Thermal and acoustic insulation.

67 **LA PEDRERA** (Passeig de Gràcia, 92)

Restoration of the façades.

89 **CASA VICENS** (Carolines, 18-24)

Restoration of the façade, bay window and patio (original tiles, sgraffito work and woodwork) and recovery of the bench-balustrade of the bay window.

FARMÀCIA ENRICH (Muntaner, 83)

Restoration and consolidation of hazardous elements and exterior façades.

77 **CASA COMALAT** (Diagonal, 442)

Restoration of the exterior façades.

9 **LONDON BAR** (Nou de la Rambla, 34)

Restoration of the interior façades of the building.

16 **MERCAT DE LA BOQUERIA** (Rambla, 91)

Restoration of the archway. Adaptation of market stalls for transformation into information points.

17 **EL INDIO** (Carme, 24)

Roof terraces of the building.

18 **BAR MUY BUENAS** (Carme, 63)

Restoration of the exterior façades.

21 **ATENEU BARCELONÈS** (Canuda, 6)

Restoration of the entrance court.

31 **CASA GOLFERICHS** (Gran Via de les Corts Catalanes, 491)

Restoration of façades and roofs, cleaning of stone walls, treatment of wood and replacement of glazed ceramics.

98 TORRE BELLESGUARD (Bellesguard, 16-20)

Start of restoration of the viaduct. Consolidation of the whole structure, lowering of the level of the earth to reveal the bottom of the pillars and landscaping of the surrounding area.

48 CASA FARGAS (Rambla de Catalunya, 47)

Light wells.

65 CASA THOMAS (Mallorca, 293)

Restoration of exterior façades.

27 RESTAURANT CASA CALVET (Casp, 48)

Improvement of hygienic conditions.

50 FARMÀCIA BOLÓS (Rambla de Catalunya, 77)

Thermal and acoustic insulation.

77 CASA COMALAT (Diagonal, 442)

Roof terraces.

75 CASA FUSTER (Passeig de Gràcia, 132)

Rehabilitation of the building for use as a hotel.

Beyond Barcelona

Local routes in Catalonia that have signed a collaboration agreement with the Barcelona Modernisme Route:

Colònia Güell, Santa Coloma de Cervelló
Jardins Artigas, La Pobla de Lillet
Manresa
Reus
Mataró-Argentona. The Puig i Cadafalch Route
Vallès Oriental, The Raspall Route
Sitges
Terrassa
Vilafranca del Penedès

These routes offer discounts to the Barcelona Modernisme Route. For further information, see the Route discount vouchers, visit www.rutadelmodernisme.com, or call the Modernisme Centre on 902 076 621.

LA COLÒNIA GÜELL

Santa Coloma de Cervelló

La Colònia Güell

La Colònia Güell

Address	Information and Welcome Centre Claudi Güell, s/n Colònia Güell 08690 Santa Coloma de Cervelló
Opening hours and visits	Monday to Saturday: November through April, 10am to 3pm May through October, 10am to 2pm and 3pm to 7pm Sundays and holidays: 10am to 3pm Guided tours to church and village are available
Information	Tel.: 936 305 807 Fax: 936 407 476 coloniaguell@terra.es
Getting there	By train: FGC from Plaça d'Espanya, trains bound for Martorell/Igualada/Manresa, running from 8.30am to 9pm (leaving every 15 minutes and taking an average of 22 minutes to get there). Tel.: 932 051 515 By car: road BV-2002 between Sant Boi de Llobregat and Santa Coloma de Cervelló
Further details	There is an introductory exhibition at the Information Centre Check updates and information on Route discount at **www.rutadelmodernisme.com** or call 902 076 621

Colònia Güell: The church (crypt) and mill village

Colònia Güell is a former mill village founded in 1890 by the bourgeois businessman and patron Eusebi Güell in Santa Coloma de Cervelló. The village was conceived, starting with the textile factory, as an urban unit of dwellings and facilities for the workers (houses, school, church, shop, club, etc.). The aim was to achieve social peace in an environment controlled by the factory owner. Colònia Güell, however, differs from other mill villages in its use of the steam engine (rather than a river) as the source of power, the separation of the factory from the residential area and the fact that it was designed by leading Modernista architects. To carry out this project Eusebi Güell hired Antoni Gaudí, Francesc Berenguer i Mestres and Joan Rubió i Bellvé. The latter two, prestigious Modernista architects and collaborators of Gaudí, were responsible for the town planning and some of the most outstanding buildings (Ca l'Ordal, Ca l'Espinal, l'Escola, Casa del Mestre, or Centre de Sant Lluís), in which they made an impressive display of the most purely Modernista architectural and decorative resources. Gaudí, on the other hand, designed the church which is popularly known as the "crypt", since only the ground floor and the portico were actually built, whereas according to the original project it was supposed to have two floors and rise 40 metres tall.

A set of Modernista buildings

Colònia Güell consists of the factory (which today houses several different firms and is in the process of being renovated), the urban centre and the church. In the Visitor's Reception Centre there is an introductory exhibition to the tour. In addition to visiting the church -with or without a guide- you can also have a guided tour of the whole village to immerse yourself in the social and creative atmosphere that existed at the start of the 20th century. After this you may like to go for a gentle stroll through the pine woods surrounding the church and feel the peace impregnating the area.

A supreme work

The Colònia Güell church crypt is regarded by many as Gaudí's masterwork. It was here that he experimented with, and succeeded in expressing, his most personal architectural language. He decided to use a system of inclined columns to bear the weight of the building without the need for buttresses or flying buttresses. He calculated the distribution of weights using a polyfunicular scale model, a method he invented for architectural design which made it possible, on a small scale, to foresee the loads and the arches that were needed to bear them. In 1969 the church was classified as a historical and artistic monument and today it is considered one of the essential pieces of 20th Century architecture in view of the major innovation consisting of the use of inclined columns and vaults in the shape of hyperbolic paraboloids and on account of the wonderful combination of materials.

The natural setting

Gaudí chose as the site for the church the highest hill in the residential part of the village amid a pine forest. As a result of the local materials used, the church and the inclined columns of the portico blend in visually with the surrounding countryside in perfect imitation of it. The walls and outer columns make use of a far-from-whimsical combination of different materials: cast iron slag, misshapen baked

bricks, calcite stone and basalt. On the outer walls there is a great profusion of mosaics with religious symbols. The portico features an impressive basalt palm tree supporting the vaults. It was in the atrium of the porch that for the first time in history Gaudí experimented with hyperbolic paroboloid vaults. There is an extraordinary mosaic on the lintel of the main door.

A startling interior

Inside the oval ground plan crypt, the main features are the solution to the ceiling, based on brick ribs, the hyperbolic paraboloid walls and the four basalt columns which have a prehistoric air about them. All this atmosphere (it must be remembered that the church was never finished) is in sharp contrast to the colours of the stained glass windows. The pews and the holy water fonts, made with enormous shell shapes supported by wrought iron, were designed by Gaudí. The shrine, the altar of the Holy Family and the angels of the presbytery are by Josep M. Jujol.

The restoration

Work on restoring the church, which is being carried out in several stages, has been in progress since September 1999. The aims of the restoration are:

- To recover the original value of the work of Antoni Gaudí, rigorously preserving the original work while eliminating the elements added after he withdrew from it.

- To finish off the work that was left incomplete, giving it a formal finish by crowning the outer wall with a material clearly differentiated from the original.

- To give the building a functional finish by improving access with a new entrance axis and new outside stairs up to the terrace roof that is the result of replacing the old, dilapidated, temporary fibrocement roof.

- To reverse the deterioration caused by the passage of time by cleaning the building, weatherproofing the ceilings and restoring the mosaics and other deteriorated items.

So far the atrium, the porches, the outside walls and the mosaics have been restored. The floor of the entrance and the floor under the porches have been renewed. The unfinished ramp which was designed to provide access to the upper nave that was never built has been restored. A new terrace roof and outside staircase have been built. The exterior lighting of the church has also been installed. The most important jobs remaining to be done are restoration of the inside of the building and improving the church's surroundings with larger grounds.

Colònia Güell Consortium

Gaudí
i la Colònia Güell
L'obra més genuïna de Gaudí en el marc d'una colònia modernista
La obra más genuina de Gaudí en el marco de una colonia modernista
Gaudí's most genuine work in the setting of a *Modernista* estate
L'œuvre la plus originale de Gaudí dans le cadre d'une colonie moderniste
Tel. 93 630 58 07
colònia güell
santa coloma de cervelló

JARDINS ARTIGAS (ARTIGAS GARDENS)

La Pobla de Lillet

The Summerhouse

Jardins Artigas

Address	Jardins artigas Parc Xesco Boix La Pobla de Lillet
Opening hours and visits	October through June: Weekends and holidays, 10am to 5pm July through September: Daily 10am to 7pm Guided visits at 12am. Private visits can be arranged all year round
Information	Tel.: 938 236 146 Fax: 938 236 414 tur.lillet@diba.es www.lillet.diba.es
Getting there	By bus: Alsina Graells company (tel. 932 656 866) By car: road C-16, or la C-17 plus C-26
Further details	Reduced price for groups and for schools Check updates and information on Route discount at **www.rutadelmodernisme.com** or call 902 076 621

Jardins Artigas (1904)

Gaudí designed the gardens known as Jardí de Can Artigas, together with a house-cum-refuge, in the nearby Serra del Catllaràs range in 1904. La Pobla de Lillet is a municipality in the comarca, or shire, of El Berguedà that has 1,558 inhabitants.

Rediscovering the work

The garden, which is private property, was abandoned from 1939 to 1989. Because of this, and the fact that the terrain is not very accessible, it remained forgotten throughout this time. Besides, the lack of documents confirming that it had actually been designed by Gaudí meant that it was not taken into consideration as part of his work. In addition to this, the house known as Xalet de Catllaràs was renovated in the 1980s with questionable criteria that made it lose all its decorative features. However, in 1991 the Càtedra Gaudí (Gaudí Chair, a univeristy research centre) began researching the two works and then tackled the project of renovating the gardens. The Chair has reconstructed a plausible hypothesis according to which it was Gaudí who designed the gardens and this has helped to make it one of the most visited points of architectural and artistic interest in El Berguedà.

A commission from Eusebi Güell

Although aesthetically there appear to be certain similarities with Park Güell, Jardins Artigas, as they are today, are the only humid gardens designed by the eminent architect.

Pont de s Arcs

At the beginning of the 20th century, the first company producing Portland cement in Spain was set up in Clot del Moro (Castellar de N'Hug). This company, Asland, was headed by the businessman Eusebi Güell i Bacigalupi. As the factory was being built (1901-1904), various service industries grew up around it, such as the coal mines in Serra del Catllaràs to feed the Asland cement furnaces. Count Güell commissioned Gaudí to design a house in Catllaràs for the engineers and professionals in charge of managing and running the coal mines.

In order to visit the place where the house was to be put up, Antoni Gaudí went to stay with the Artigas family who were in the textile business. During the two days he spent in La Pobla, they told him that they would very much like to have a garden behind their factory. Out of gratitude for the family's hospitality, Antoni Gaudí made them a sketch. It is from this sketch that Jardins Artigas came into being.

Similarities with Park Güell

It should be said that in 1905 Gaudí was working in Barcelona on the construction of Park Güell, so the sketch he made of the garden took its inspiration from this park. It seems that when he returned to Barcelona with the design for the Xalet de Catllaràs, Gaudí himself sent two workers to La Pobla de Lillet to start work on the garden he had drawn.

Picnic bench

A wild environment

The place where Jardins Artigas were built is in a very wild environment with the river Llobregat running between large jagged rocks and abundant indigenous vegetation. The architectural structures are the same as in Park Güell, but the materials used to build the garden were taken from the mountainous area near the Pyrenees where La Pobla de Lillet is situated. Therefore the materials you will see in the garden are stone slabs, pumice stone, pebbles from the river and marl, together with Portland cement which was used for the garden's balustrades and naturalistic murals.

Pont d'Escala

Eagle and summerhouse

Besides the Llobregat river, there are plenty of water sources, with a large number of fountains spouting from the springs of natural water running down to the river. All that Gaudí did was to decorate them and make them into fountains with figures from which they take their names, such as La Cascada (The Waterfall), Font del Bou (Bull Fountain), Font del Lleó (The Lion Fountain) and Font de la Gruta (Grotto Fountain). The bridges, Pont d'Escala and Pont dels Arcs, were built to provide a way across the Llobregat and link the two banks of the river. Standing on a

The Grotto

pronounced blade of rock overlooking the whole garden is La Glorieta, a summerhouse with a magnificent view.

There are various symbols to look out for in the garden such as the Four Evangelists presided over by the figure of an eagle majestically watching over the garden from the side of the Glorieta del Bou (Bull's Summerhouse), the lion and the Angel, which originally stood inside the waterfall, but has not been reproduced. Snakes protect the only entrance Gaudí designed for the garden. Other points of interest include the caryatides with the figure of man and woman, the fisherman's corner, the picnic area with its naturalistic mural and the bamboo reeds.

Font del Bou

Pont dels Arcs

Ajuntament de La Pobla de Lillet
(La Pobla de Lillet Town Council)

Manresa

Address	Tourist Office Via de Sant Ingnasi, 40, ground floor
Opening hours and visits	In winter: Tuesday to Friday 9am to 4pm; Saturday 10am to 2pm and 5pm to 8pm; Sunday 10am to 2pm. In summer: Tuesday to Friday 9am to 2pm and 5pm to 7pm; Saturday 10am to 2pm and 5pm to 8pm; Sunday 10am to 2pm Guided visits every first Saturday of the month: visits last about two hours and must be booked in advance.
Information	Tel.: 938 784 090 Fax: 938 784 156 turisme@ajmanresa.org www.ajmanresa.org
Getting there	By train: RENFE and FGC, both leaving from Palaça Catalunya. By bus: Autocars Julià company (tel.: 934 026 937). By car: road C-58 to Terrassa, then C-16 or C-55 to Manresa
Further details	Reduced prices for groups. If you prefer to walk the visit on your own, the Tourist Office gives out free maps of Manresa's Modernisme. Check updates and information on Route discount at **www.rutadelmodernisme.com** or call 902 076 621

During the 19th century, Manresa, like other small towns and villages along the rivers Llobregat and Cardener, grew into an industrial town. The first textile factories appeared and, as a result, the first lineages of businessmen. The town was transformed. The last of the walls around it were pulled down and much wider streets were built. Passeig Pere III, opened during the 19th century, became the favourite residential avenue of the new bourgeoisie. The industrialists who had made their fortune thanks to the textile mills, had houses built there that followed the Modernista aesthetics. Most of these buildings were designed by local architects who took their cue from the dominant trend in Barcelona. Of these, two in particular stood out: Ignasi Oms i Ponsa and Alexandre Soler i March. Ignasi Oms is regarded as the foremost representative of Modernisme in Manresa. He worked with Domènech i Montaner and for many years was the municipal architect. Manresa is full of his buildings and there is even a street named after him, which contains four of his works. Like Ignasi Oms, Alexandre Soler trained in Barcelona and was also disciple of Domènech i Montaner. One of the most important works for which he was responsible was the extension of Santa Clara Convent.

Modernista Route

The Modernista route is centred mainly on the area of Plaça Sant Domènec, Passeig Pere III and Carrer del Born.

Plaça de Sant Domènec

Farmàcia Esteve (1926) and Quiosc de l'Arpa (1917)

These are clear examples of Modernisme as applied to shops and urban furniture. They were designed by the architect Josep Firmat. It is worth noting the stained glass windows and the wood and wrought iron sculptures of the chemists'.

Quiosc de l'Arpa

Sastreria Tuneu

This tailors' shop still boasts the Modernista signs designed by the painter Francesc Cuixart in 1906.

Casa Torrents or *Buresa*

This building was designed by Ignasi Oms in 1905, a commission by one of the wealthiest families of the time, the Torrents. It is a re-creation of a palatial house in Neo-Gothic style with four storeys and a tower on either side of it. A central body juts out of the façade with a large enclosed balcony on the first floor and four pinnacles and an image of the Holy Family, a typical feature of many Modernista buildings, at the top. Some of the rooms still retain their luxurious Modernista decoration.

Casal Regionalista

Designed by Alexandre Soler in 1918. With its sober, regular style it moves away from the Modernista postulates and closer to those of the movement known as Noucentisme.

Casino

Situated right in the middle of Passeig Pere III, it is the main Modernista building in Manresa. Designed by Ignasi Oms, it was constructed in 1906. It was known as *El Casino dels senyors* (the Gentlemen's Casino) as it functioned as a social club and gambling place for the well-to-do of the time. The Casino closed during the sixties and the building went into a period of decline. Later on, however, it was bought by the local authority and today houses a public library and a cultural centre.

The Casino is a transitional work on the way to fully-fledged Modernisme. The façade has a classical structure, although it also contains Modernista elements such as the windows, balconies and ornamental motifs. Some of the rooms inside it, now used as reading rooms, still have their original stained glass windows and extremely rich ornamentation.

Casino

Casa Lluvià

Casa Lluvià

Designed by Ignasi Oms in 1908, it is regarded as the purest example of Modernista architecture in Manresa. Unlike the Casino, Casa Lluvià moves away from classicism and here the architect combines a central body with two towers of different proportions and heights. The façade retains its typically Modernista ornamentation while the interior of the building has also kept some Modernista elements such as the stone columns with naïf-style reliefs and paintings. It is currently home to the Bages i Berguedà Architects' Association.

Casa Torra

Designed by Ignasi Oms in 1910, it stands out because it succeeds in the idea of a detached house that is nevertheless perfectly integrated into the urban space.

Casa Gabernet Espanyol

Designed by Ignasi Oms in 1898. This is an example of historicist Modernisme combining Gothic and Romanesque elements.

MANRESA
CIUTAT MIL·LENÀRIA

La seducció del Modernisme

Visites guiades a la Manresa modernista
Visitas guiadas a la Manresa modernista
Guided tours to the Modernist route in Manresa
Visites guidées à l'itineraire d'Art Nouveau de Manresa

Cada primer dissabte de mes
Cada primer sábado de mes
Every first Saturday of the month
Tous les premiers samedis du mois

Reserves a:
Reservas en, Bookings at, Réservations à

Oficina de Turisme de Manresa
Via de Sant Ignasi, 40, baixos
08240 Manresa
Tel. 93 878 40 90
Correu-e: turisme@ajmanresa.org

Casa Padró

This building was designed in 1918 by Bernat Pejoan and stands on a corner of Passeig Pere III. It now contains shops.

Casa Padró Domènech

Designed by Ignasi Oms in 1903.

Col·legi Asil dels Infants

Designed by Ignasi Oms and built between 1901 and 1911 it falls within the realm of historicist Modernisme.

Casa Armengou

Designed by Ignasi Oms in 1889. It is a mixture of eclectic and Modernista styles.

Institut Lluís de Peguera

Designed by Alexandre Soler. It is regarded as belonging to the Modernista style in transition towards Noucentisme. Work on it began in 1907, but it was not completed until 1927.

Convent de Santa Clara

This is a building of medieval origin and it still has a Romanesque doorway. In 1904 the architect Alexandre Soler designed an extension to the building drawing his inspiration from the Gothic.

Oficina de Turisme de Manresa. Ajuntament de Manresa
(Manresa Tourist Office. Manresa City Council)

Reus, a Modernista stage

Reus, Gaudí's city, 100 kilometres from Barcelona and eight from the Costa Daurada, is today a major commercial and cultural hub of the south of Catalonia.

In the 18th century, the population of the town grew rapidly to become the second largest city in Catalonia as the result of the brandy trade, for which it was an international reference point, as evidenced by the famous joke-phrase of an alleged "Reus, París i Londres (London)" axis. It was shortly after this, around the end of the 19th and the beginning of the 20th century, that the great Modernista buildings, which you can still see today and which make Reus a veritable Modernista stage, were erected.

Reus	
Address	Oficina de Turisme Carrer Sant Joan, 34
Opening hours and visits	The Reus Tourism Department organizes guided visits to the city's heritage and opens to the public buildings which are usually closed to visits. A single ticket includes two different guided visits and free entrance to the Salvador Vilaseca Museum, the "Gaudi & Reus" exhibition and the Reus Art and History Museum. From October through June visits are on Saturday (if not a holiday) at 11am, and must be booked in advance. From July through September there are several daily visits, morning and afternoon. No visits on Sunday and on August 15th and September 25th. Private group visits may be booked in advance all year round.
Information	Tel.: 977 778 149 infoturisme@reus.net www.reus.net/turisme
Getting there	By train: RENFE from Sants and Passeig de Gràcia stations. By bus: La Hispano Igualadina company (tel.: 938 044 451), leaving from Ronda Universitat. By car: road N-340 or highway AP-7 (exit no. 34)
Further details	The guided visit is a walking tour to see the façades of the main Modernista buildings and includes access to the interior of Casa Gasull, the garden of Casa Rull and the shop of Casa Navàs, all by Lluis Domènech i Montaner. Then a bus ride takes you to Hospital Pere Mata where you visit pavillion 6. Also by Domènech, the decorative richness of this hospital is especially noteworthy in this pavillion. Entrance to Casa Navàs depends on the owners' availability:it is an optional visit not included in the ticket. Check updates and information on Route discount at **www.rutadelmodernisme.com** or call 902 076 621

The universally famous architect Antoni Gaudí i Cornet was born in Reus on 25th June 1852. It was in this city that the future architect lived as a child and teenager, made friends and went to school before moving to Barcelona. Some of his closest collaborators, such as the architects Joan Rubió i Bellvé, Domènec Sugranyes and Francesc Berenguer, and several of his future clients also came from the Reus area.

The city still retains the memory of the places the young Gaudí frequented during the time he lived in the town: the house where he was born, the church where he was baptised, the school he went to, the places where he used to meet his friends and collaborators. In short, the streets, squares, places and landscapes of the city that shaped the education of its great creative genius.

We suggest you also visit the "Gaudí & Reus" exhibition at the **Museu Salvador Vilaseca** which takes you through the origins of Gaudí and his family and introduces you to some of the most significant aspects of his personality and his way of understanding the world and architecture.

But it was the arrival of Lluís Domènech i Montaner, the other great architect of the era, that marked the start of the brilliant Modernista period in Reus when he began the plans to build the **Pere Mata Psychiatric Institute** in 1898. This was followed by other commissions and it was in Reus that Lluís Domènech i Montaner constructed more buildings than anywhere else apart from Barcelona. Of these, the most important are:

Pere Mata Institute (1898)

An innovative construction project involving an interesting combination of materials featuring brick, stone, wrought iron, ceramic and stained glass, and an innovative approach to patient care, in which the architect used a system of independent pavilions, something he repeated later on at the Hospital de Sant Pau in Barcelona. Pavilion number six, with its rich ornamentation, is the most valuable from an artistic point of view, as it retains its spectacular original Modernista decorative repertoire. The Pere Mata Institute, whose interior you can visit, is regarded as one of the jewels of Catalan Modernisme.

Pere Mata Institute

Casa Navàs (1901-1907)

Together with the Pere Mata Institute, this is the best example of the city's architecture. It was commissioned by Joaquim Navàs, a local merchant. The beautiful façade, with different architectural and decorative elements inspired by Gothic and Plateresque, was damaged by a bomb during the Civil War, but the interior still keeps its magnificent decoration. The shop on the ground floor of the building is also very interesting, as the construction has survived virtually intact, and you can look round inside it.

Casa Rull (1900)

This house was designed for Pere Rull, a notary, and you can recognise various symbols on the façade to do with the original owner's profession. Of special note are the angle formed by the two main façades and the elegant balcony with floral elements on the first floor. You can also visit the garden of this house.

Casa Rull

Reus
LA CIUTAT DE GAUDÍ
T'obrim
les
portes
del
modernisme
Te abrimos las puertas del Modernisme
Nous ouvrons les portes du Modernisme
We open the doors of Modernisme for you
PATRONAT MUNICIPAL
DE TURISME I COMERÇ
REUS
VISITES GUIADES
Oficina de Turisme
Informació i reserves: 977 778 149
www.reus.net/turisme

Casa Gasull (1911)

This house was built for Fèlix Gasull, the owner of an oil-exporting firm, and contained the company's warehouses as well as the family dwelling. This building is an early example of Modernisme combined with an incipient and sober *Noucentisme*.

There is no doubt that Modernista buildings erected in Reus were influenced by the architectural style of Domènech i Montaner. This effect is specially evident in the works designed by Pere Caselles, a municipal architect who had already worked with Domènech on the **Pere Mata Institute** and who designed a large number of both public and private buildings, including the **Prat de la Riba Schools** (1911), **Casa Grau** (1910), **Casa Sagarra** (1908), **Casa Munné** (1904), **Casa Laguna** (1904), **Casa Tomàs Jordi** (1909) and **Casa Punyed** (1900), and various industrial buildings such as the **Abbatoir** (begun by Francesc Borràs in 1889), and the **Oenological Station** (1906). Of the other architects who worked in Reus during this period, the most important were Joan Rubió i Bellvé, who was influenced by Gaudí's style (**Xalet Serra**, 1911; **Tuberculosis Dispensary**, 1926, and **Casa Serra**, 1924), and Pere Domènech i Roura, the son of Domènech i Montaner (**Casa Marco**, 1926).

Patronat Municipal de Turisme i Comerç de Reus
(Reus Municipal Board of Tourism and Trade)

Ruta Puig i Cadafalch

Modernisme was a social and political movement of great magnitude with a major impact on the arts that spread throughout Catalonia, at the same time as it did across the rest of Europe and America (where it was more commonly known as Art Nouveau or the New Style), between the final third of the 19th century and the first quarter of the 20th century. In Catalonia it made itself felt not only in the big cities, but also in other towns such as Mataró, Argentona and Canet de Mar whose historical and social characteristics made

Ruta Puig i Cadafalch

Address	Museu de Mataró Carreró, 17-19 08301 Mataró
Opening hours and visits	Tickets are sold at the Museum, open Monday, Wednesday and Friday 10am to 1pm. Guided visits start at 10am and end at 1.30pm. Available in Catalan, Spanish, English, French and German (must be pre-arranged). Urban parts of the Route are done on foot, and the distance between towns is done by bus. Maximum people per group is thirty people; minimum needed to arrange a private tour is twenty people. Scheduled tours are every first and third weekend of the month.
Information	Actium Patrimoni Cultural, SL info@actiumweb.com Tel.: 639 566 887 Monday, Wednesday and Friday from 10am to 1pm
Getting there	By train: RENFE - Trains bound for Blanes or Mataró, from Sants and Plaça Catalunya stations. By bus: Casa company (tel.: 937 981 100) leaving from Ronda Universitat. By car: C-32 northbound (exit no. 11)
Further details	Check updates and information on Route discount at **www.rutadelmodernisme.com** or call 902 076 621 The Puig i Cadafalch Route includes guided visit to several buildings by the architect. In Mataró you will see the Town Hall, with its beautiful Modernista ceilings; the house where Puig was born; the Rengle market; the La Confianza shop; the Casa Parera, the building of La Beneficència and the Casa Coll i Regàs (now Fundació Caixa Laietana), in which the best interiors are seen. Next, a bus takes you to Argentona, where you will see the architect and politician's summer residence; the chapel of Sacrament (Sant Julià church); the country manor Can Calopa and the magnificent Can Garí, one of the outstanding examples of Puig i Cadafalch's work

them ideal places for such trends to manifest themselves. Architecture was the most representative form taken by these changes in style and ways of living, as it constituted a set of highly visible "modernities" encompassing both structure and the applied arts.

The Maresme shire developed dynamically into a broad range of productive sectors, mainly textiles and glass, liqueurs and wine-growing, while at the same time becoming a place where the Catalan bourgeoisie spent its summers and took the waters (the hot-water springs of Caldes d'Estrac and the medicinal springs of Argentona). It also attracted sailors and merchants returning from the Americas with the intention of settling down for good where they had originally come from.

Some of the creators of the architectural projects of Modernisme, such as Josep Puig i Cadafalch, Eduard Ferrés i Puig, Emili Cabanyes and Ignasi Mas i Morell, came from the Maresme, while others, such as Lluís Domènech i Montaner and Antoni M. Gallissà, made it their home. Their works display a rich variety of architectural types ranging from large summer residences, industrial buildings (factories, wine cellars) and shops to public commissions (town halls, markets, schools, abattoirs, children's homes, churches, etc.). Josep Puig i Cadafalch and Lluís Domènech i Montaner were two of the leading exponents of Modernisme in Catalonia and were responsible for the fact that the Maresme has one of this movement's most notable architectural heritages. In 2001, Mataró and Argentona, together with Barcelona, organised the Josep Puig i Cadafalch Year with various activities covering different cultural manifestations with a view to raising awareness about him and his outstanding work.

Mataró

Saló de Sessions de l'Ajuntament (1893), La Riera, 48. In 1893, Puig i Cadafalch, who at that time was working as a municipal architect in Mataró, drew up the plans for the renovation of the Sessions Hall in the town hall. Of particular note is the decoration of the panelled ceiling with beams adorned with coats-of-arms and emblematic symbols crossing each other.

The house where Puig i Cadafalch was born, El Carreró, 39. This house is an 18th century building known locally as a *casa de cós*, a long and narrow terraced house. A commemorative plaque on the façade, put up in 1967, recalls the figure of the illustrious architect. The façade was restored in 2001 on the occasion of Puig i Cadafalch Year.

El Rengle (1891-1893), Plaça Gran, s/n. The plans for this market building were drawn up by Emili Cabanyes, the municipal architect at that time. Puig i Cadafalch was responsible for renovating the semicircular roof decorated with ceramic tiles, open brickwork and wrought iron ornamental details.

El Rengle Market

La Confianza (1894-1896), Carrer de Sant Cristòfor, 10. This shop was commissioned by Francesc Palomer and opened in 1896. It sold pasta for soup and olive oil. Inside, the walls and ceiling of the shop are decorated with vegetable motifs and ornamental friezes and there are display cabinets with Neo-Gothic-style pinnacles, while outside it features a wrought iron sign with Modernista lettering.

La Confianza

Inside La Confianza

Casa Parera (1894), Carrer Nou, 20. This building was renovated for Miquel Parera i Partagàs. It is a former two-storey casa de cós with floral and vegetable sgraffiti, exposed brickwork, wrought iron and medieval-type sculptural elements (corbels, coats-of-arms and gargoyles).

Casa Parera

La Beneficència (1894), Carrer Sant Josep, 9. La Casa de la Beneficència, to give it its full name, was a poorhouse in the former Carmelite convent of Sant Josep, occupied at that time by the Conceptionists. Puig broke up the austere façade with large windows with corolla columns and medieval-inspired capitals, Neo-Gothic-style sculptural elements and the coats-of-arms of Mataró and Catalonia.

La Beneficència

Casa Coll i Regàs

Casa Coll i Regàs (1896-1898), Carrer d'Argentona, 55-57. This house was commissioned by the Mataró businessman Joaquim Coll i Regàs. It is currently the headquarters of Fundació Caixa Laietana and the most emblematic Modernista building in town. In this building Puig i Cadafalch marshalled a comprehensive range of iconography and decoration with the intention of flattering his client, a prestigious textile industrialist.

Argentona

Puig i Cadafalch's summer residence

Puig i Cadafalch's summer residence (1897-1905), Plaça de Vendre, s/n. This is the house where the architect used to spend the summer when he was little and where he later found refuge upon his return from exile in 1942. Puig opened up the party walls so as to join up what were originally three separate dwellings and make them into one. Of particular note are the Modernista elements such as the battlements, the sculptures and the broken-tile decoration (known as trencadís) on the chimneys.

Capella del Sagrament (1896-1897), Plaça de l'Església, 1. The new chapel is in Neo-Gothic style. It can be reached through a side door from the church of Sant Julià. The nave of the chapel has a rectangular ground plan, while the apse is built on a semi-hexagonal ground plan and roofed with lancet-arch vaults.

Can Calopa (1898), Carrer de Riudemeia, 8. This sixteenth-century manor house and ancestral home occupies four cóssos and has a pyramidal roof. According to Lluís Bonet i Garí, the plans for alterations to the building, which gave it its eclectic appearance, were drawn up by Puig i Cadafalch.

Casa Garí

Casa Garí (1898), Camí de Sant Miquel del Cros, 9. This former Catalan country house was converted into a Nordic-inspired mansion for use as a summer residence in just nine months. Puig i Cadafalch was commissioned by Josep Garí i Cañas to take care of the architectural side of the transformation. Casa Garí was turned into veritable palace combining every luxury and facility (a theatre, gardens, a lake) with the image of a solid, fortified country house (two watchtowers facing south and a tower, with a sgraffito sundial on the wall, attached to the house).

Torre d'Aigües del Cros (1900), Avinguda Molí de les Mateves, s/n. This circular water-raising tower, shaped like a chimney, is made of clay bricks and has a roof decorated with broken tiles or *trencadís*. It supplied water to the Can Garí estate.

Torre d'Aigües del Cros

After this, the minibus takes you back to Mataró where the tour ends in Plaça de les Tereses.

Ajuntament d'Argentona
(Argentona Town Coucil)
Ajuntament de Mataró
(Mataró Town Council)
Actium Patrimoni Cultural, SL

Ruta Puig i Cadafalch

Mataró - Argentona

THE RASPALL ROUTE, VALLÈS ORIENTAL

A suggestion for discovering the architecture of the summer residences in Vallès Oriental and the work of the architect Manuel Joaquim Raspall (1877-1954) in L'Ametlla, Cardedeu, La Garriga and Granollers.

The Modernisme of Summer Residences in Vallès Oriental: The Raspall Route

At the end of the 19th century, El Vallès Oriental was a shire that still had a strong agricultural base and timid industrial growth, highly focused on the capital, Granollers. However, its proximity to Barcelona and improved communication routes -local roads and two railway lines linking Barcelona to France- were at one and the same time key factors in triggering a process of development and transformation, and the cause and consequence

Ruta Raspall

Address	Museu-Arxiu Tomàs Balvey Daurella, 1 08004 Cardedeu
Opening hours and visits	Two main choices are available: One-day tour in l'Ametlla, la Garriga and Cardedeu, on the last Sunday of every month, from March to October. Tours start at 9.30am and end at 6pm. Guide, transport and entrance fees included. Half-a-day tour in l'Ametlla and la Garriga, or Cardedeu and Granollers. Available all year round, if booked in advance. Tours start at 10am and end at 2pm. Guide and entrance fees included (breakfast, lunch and transport are optional).
Information	Tel.: 938 713 070 / 639 566 887 (Pilar Vera) Fax: 938 711 477 m.cardedeu@diba.es www.museudecardedeu.org www.truismevalles.net
Getting there	By train: RENFE, trains bound for Girona or Maçanet from Sants or Passeig de Gràcia stations. By bus: Sagalés company (tel.: 938 707 860). By car: road C-58 or highway AP-7 (exit Cardedeu)
Further details	Custom-made tours are available all year round if booked in advance. Minimum twenty people per group. Special guided tours in sign language also available. Check updates and information on Route discount at www.rutadelmodernisme.com or call 902 076 621

Raspall's signature

of a phenomenon that characterised the small towns and villages of this area until well into the 20th century: the custom of city-dwellers to move out of Barcelona for the summer.

From the middle of the 19th century onwards, this practice grew into a new form of leisure for the better-off classes in the cities, especially Barcelona. Although it began under the guise of therapeutic stays, by the 20th century it was simply a matter of people finding places away, but not too far, from their habitual residences, where they could engage in social life and enjoy a long period of holidays. The small towns and villages of El Vallès such as L'Ametlla, La Garriga and Cardedeu, which had hung on to their rural and agrarian character, gradually became attractive places to spend the summer on account of their nearness to Barcelona, their countryside and, above all, their therapeutic resources.

Doctors, lawyers, industrialists, financiers, politicians, people returning from the Americas having made their fortune and even artists, mainly from Barcelona, formed an emerging social class that was by no means compact, but had its own habits and ways of life defining it as a class. One of these habits was to go and spend the summer in places where they constituted a colony of summer residents. The colony was a clearly differentiated group within the life of each municipality. They dressed mainly in white, with parasols, hats, fans and sunglasses, frequented the Casino, the colony's social hub and meeting point as well as an essential facility in every summer resort, and organised a range of activities, from dances and parties, plays and literary evenings to concerts, gymkhanas and excursions, not to mention all kinds of public and private events. Some of these were much talked-about, such as the two performances, including the première of the play *La viola d'or* (The Golden Viola) by Apel·les Mestres with music by Enric Morera, at the Teatre de la Natura in the Can Terres wood in La Garriga in 1911 and 1914, and the performance of the operetta *Maruja* by Amadeu Vives, in 1915, in the Vilalba wood in Cardedeu.

For small towns and villages such as L'Ametlla, La Garriga and Cardedeu, the summer residence phenomenon brought with it a considerable economic awakening that

Casa Millet

stimulated trade, direct relations with Barcelona, the development of services such as inns and spas and, above all, a boost to new construction and urban growth. The colony of summer residents needed new houses to stay in, either as owners or for rent, and these buildings had to incorporate the latest architectural trends of the time: Modernisme.

In L'Ametlla, La Garriga and Cardedeu magnificent homes were built in the Modernista style with lush gardens that today stand as testimony to a particular period. In these towns there are a large number of buildings, principally summer residences, by renowned architects of the time such as Eduard M. Balcells, Puig i Cadafalch, Jeroni Martorell, Emili Sala i Cortés and, above all, Joaquim Raspall, who had family connections with La Garriga. M.J. Raspall i Mayol (1877-1954), a disciple of Domènech i Montaner and Puig i Cadafalch, is regarded as belonging to the second generation of Modernista architects. Most of his work, with a markedly singular style, is to be found in the small towns in El Vallès for which he worked as a municipal architect - in Cardedeu (1904), L'Ametlla del Vallès (1906), La Garriga (1906), Granollers (1907), Caldes de Montbui (1909) and later Montmeló (1924). In these municipalities he built remarkable houses in the Modernista style as well as carrying out public-sector works, including town planning, designs for urban furniture and even **Cardedeu Municipal Cemetery**.

Going round these towns will give you the chance to get to know Raspall's Modernista architecture, evoke the time when the practice of moving residence for the summer was in fashion and discover municipalities that were transformed and acquired character in the early part of the 20th century. The suggested route, entitled The Modernisme of Summer Residences in El Vallès Oriental: The Raspall Route, will allow you to spend a whole day going through L'Ametlla, La Garriga and Cardedeu discovering interesting corners, singular buildings and above all Modernista architecture designed for people to spend and enjoy their summers in Vallès Oriental.

The guided tour sets off from Cardedeu at half past nine in the morning. It begins with a brief coach trip to L'Ametlla del Vallès, a small town of medieval origin that became a centre for summer residences in the early 20th century. The main feature of the visit to L'Ametlla is **Casa Millet**, a 14th century farmhouse that was converted by Raspall in 1908 into the summer residence of Joan Millet, a cotton industrialist and brother of Lluís Millet, director and joint founder of the Catalan choral society, L'Orfeó Català. The garden, the façade and the interesting fireplace in the dining room are testimony to the architect's most Modernista period.

After a guided walk and time for a coffee, the route continues to La Garriga, a watering place ever since Roman times and the town where most of the Modernista architecture in El Vallès Oriental is concentrated. A selection of over twenty houses will take you back to the time when it was the fashion to move out of the city in the summer, and give you the chance to enjoy the garden of **Casa Barbey** (1910), a house which the textile industrialist Juli Barbey built and is today one of the foremost examples of the Modernista movement outside the Barcelona area. Casa Barbey and the neighbouring buildings of **Torre Iris** (1911), **La Bombonera** (1910) and **Casa Barraquer** (1912-13) form the so-called **Illa Raspall**, or Raspall Block, a unique set of buildings in Catalonia now listed as of National Interest.

From La Garriga you go back to Cardedeu, stopping off at the municipal cemetery, one of the most interesting and remarkable pieces of funereal architecture in Catalonia. After an optional lunch, the route continues through the centre of Cardedeu with visits to **Alqueria Cloelia** (1904), the first private-sector work by Raspall, the **gardens of Casa Viader** (1917-1922), commissioned by Marc Viader, the inventor of Cacaolat, the locally famous chocolate drink, and an exclusive visit to the entrance hall and library of **Casa Golferichs-Rovellat** (1908), which boasts a noteworthy set of glasswork with leaded stained-glass windows featuring completely Modernista figures and patterns.

Casa Clapés

The route is open to all types of groups and individuals and has special educational variants for school parties.

Modernisme d'Estiueig al Vallès Oriental (The Modernisme of Summer Residences in El Vallès Oriental)
Ajuntament de l'Ametlla (L'Ametlla Town Council)
Ajuntament de Cardedeu (Cardedeu Town Council)
Ajuntament de la Garriga (La Garriga Town Council)
Ajuntament de Granollers (Granollers Town Council)
Consorci de Turisme del Vallès Oriental (Vallès Oriental Tourist Board)

Modernisme d´estiueig al Vallès Oriental

rutaRaspall

Consorci de turisme del Vallès Oriental

Modernisme d'Estiueig al Vallès Oriental

...ntament de l'Ametlla del Vallès
Ajuntament de Cardedeu
Ajuntament de la Garriga
Ajuntament de Granollers

Diputació Barcelona
xarxa de municipis

TurismeTotal

Informació / Information:
Museu Arxiu Tomàs Balvey
Dr. Daurella, 1. Cardedeu
Tel. 93.871.30.70
m.cardedeu@diba.es

Itineraris guiats/
Guided Tours

www.museudecardedeu.org
www.turismevalles.net

Casal Dr. Daurella
Museu Arxiu Tomàs Balvey
Cardedeu

SITGES

For Sitges , the 19th century was a period of prosperity full of social, economic, technological and cultural changes, as it was for the rest of the Garraf shire, of which it is a part. The arrival of the railway, the export of wine by sea, the South American adventure, urban development and the bourgeoning of architectural styles made a major impact on this small Catalan coastal town.

Between 1892 and 1899 Sitges became a meeting place for Modernista artists following the arrival of Santiago Rusiñol i Prats in 1891. The painter (Barcelona 1861 - Aranjuez 1931), settled down to live here in Cau Ferrat having been attracted by the town's scenary, by its inhabitants and by the colony of painters belonging to the Luminist school that already existed there.

Sitges

Address	Oficina Maricel Fonollar, s/n 08870 Sitges Oficina Oasis Sinia Morera, 1 08870 Sitges
Opening hours and visits	Maricel Office: Monday to Friday, from 9am to 2pm and 4pm to 6.30pm. From June through September, daily from 9am to 9pm . Scheduled visits on the first Sunday of every month. Visits only start if the group is at least 15 people. Entrance fee to the museum included. Groups may book private visits for any day all year round. There is no minimum of people in this option and language may be chosen beforehand, but entrance fee to the museum is not included in the price
Information	Modernista tour information and bookings: Tel.: 619 793 199 agis_sitges@hotmail.com General Tourist information at Maricel Office: Tel.: 938 110 611 www.sitgestur.com Oasis office (hotel bookings): Tel.: 938 944 251 Fax: 938 944 305
Getting there	By train: RENFE trains bound for Vilanova or Sant Vicenç de Calders, from Sants or Passeig de Gràcia stations. By bus: Mon Bus company (tel.: 938 937 060) leaving from Ronda Universitat. By car: toll road C-32 (Garraf tunnels) or road C-31
Further details	Check updates and information on Route discount at **www.rutadelmodernisme.com** or call 902 076 621

Having been taken into their midst by these painters, Rusiñol organised five Festes Modernistes (Modernista Festivals) that brought the leading writers, musicians, critics, sculptors and artists in Catalonia to Sitges and turned this small seafaring town into "the Mecca of Modernisme" as it came to be called. In the summer of 1892, the First Fine Arts Exhibition, subsequently known as the First Modernista Festival, was held in the town hall. The exhibition included works by local artists, Ramon Casas, Eliseu Meifrèn and Santiago Rusiñol, all of whom were very significant figures in the Modernista movement.

The Modernista artists were keen to open themselves up to Europe and its cultural movements and Rusiñol and the group around the magazine *L'Avenç* organised the Second Modernista Festival with this object in mind. Taking the Belgian creators as reference point and in close collaboration with Enric Morera, who had trained as an artist in Brussels, they staged *The Intruder*, a work by the young Belgian playwright Maeterlinck, at the Casino Prado theatre. Music featured prominently at this Festival and there was a concert with works by César Frank and Enric Morera.

Josep Reynés, 1897-1898 - *El Greco*

The Third Modernista Festival, borne along by confidence in the victory of Modernista ideals, was held in November 1894 and was very different from the other two. The events comprising the Festival were a procession bringing two paintings by Doménikos Theotokópoulos, El Greco, to Sitges and the official opening of Cau Ferrat, Rusiñol's studio. The procession, organised by Rusiñol, was a demonstration of the excitement Rusiñol and his friends experienced at the sight of the works by El Greco, which they felt they had to show in popular fashion. These paintings, which Rusiñol bought from Pau Bosch in Paris, are now in the Cau Ferrat Museum. Once Cau Ferrat had been officially opened, a lunch was held nearby, at La Torreta, on the rocks, and then, after a speech by Rusiñol, a literary competition began during which Joan Maragall recited his "decadentist" verses, which were later to be regarded as the beginning of a new genre of poetry.

Music was the star of the Fourth Modernista Festival which took place on 14 February 1897, this time returning to the Casino Prado where a portrait of Enric Morera by Santiago Rusiñol hung in the foyer. The events began with a symphonic

Casino Prado Suburense
Detail of the façade

poem by Mercè Vidal, and the *Canadian Dances* by Paul Gibson, following which Rusiñol made a speech defending Modernista music. The Festival ended with the première of the opera *La Fada* (*The Fairy*), with a libretto by Jaume Massó i Torrents and music by Enric Morera. This was the most important event of the Fourth Modernista Festival.

The Fifth Modernista Festival, held in August 1899, staged two plays by Ignasi Iglésias, *Lladres* (*Thieves*) and *La reina del cor* (*The Queen of the Heart*), and one by Santiago Rusiñol, *L'alegria que passa* (*Passing Joy*). The pianist Joaquim Nin played works by Scarlatti, Grieg, Alió, Gay and Morera.

Sitges Modernista Route

The Modernista Route allows you to discover the imprint Modernisme left on Sitges as a result of the initiatives by Santiago Rusiñol and the wealth of the so-called *americanos*

Casa Bonaventura Blay, Villa Avelina

- local people who returned from the Spanish colonies having made their fortunes and embellished the streets of the town with their Modernista-style houses.

The Route begins at the train station, the symbol of the new era and the country's modernity. It continues along the streets running through the town centre -Carrer de l'Illa de Cuba and Carrer de Francesc Gumà- where you can discover the Modernista constructions of some of the most outstanding architects of the time, such as Gaietà Buïgas, and where you can enjoy the decoration of some of the frontages (wrought iron work, ceramics, sgrafitti, stained glass windows, etc.). The buildings here include

Casa Manuel Planas

Casa Bonaventura Blay (1901), **Casa Manuel Planas** (1908) and **Casa Pere Carreras** (1906). If at all possible, you should take a look inside the **Teatre Prado**, a Modernista building where two of the Modernista Festivals organised by Rusiñol in Sitges were held and a meeting point for many of those involved.

The Route continues with a visit to a blue courtyard, the sole surviving example of the once typical Sitges courtyards, which was a source of inspiration for Rusiñol, who not only painted several pictures of it, but also based a play on it entitled *El pati blau* (The Blue Courtyard). You continue along Cap de la Vila to see another of the Modernista houses, one that once belonged to the *americano* Bartomeu Carbonell i Mussons. Next you come to Plaça de l'Ajuntament where the principal constructions are the Town Hall, featuring a Neo-Gothic style much used by the Modernista artists, and the market, the first Modernista building in Sitges.

The visit ends at the **Cau Ferrat Museum**, which was once the house-cum-studio of artist and art collector Santiago Rusiñol. Inside there is a large number of paintings by El Greco, Ramon Casas, Ignacio Zuloaga, Picasso and Rusiñol, among many others, as well as an extensive collection of wrought iron, ceramic and glass items.

Patronat Municipal de Turisme de Sitges
(Sitges Municipal Tourist Board)

Casa Bartomeu Carbonell

Ruta Cultural Sitges en el temps del Modernisme
Ruta Cultural Sitges en la época del Modernismo
Route Culturelle Sitges au temps du Modernisme
Cultural Trail Sitges at the time of *Modernisme*

Industrial and Modernista Terrassa

The origins of the industrial transformation of Terrassa go back to the first third of the 19th century and have to do mainly with the expansion of the woollen textile industry. Technical improvements began with the introduction of spinning machines (1832) and steam engines (1833). Not long after this, from 1845 onwards, came the Jacquard looms that were to play a key part in the expansion of the textile industry. This development was aided by improved transport, including the building of a new road to Barcelona in 1845, but particularly by the arrival of the northern railway in 1856 linking Terrassa to Barcelona, Manresa and Saragossa. This new means of transport made it easier for raw materials, such as coal and wool, to be brought in and for the finished textile products to be sent out to the markets of Catalonia and the rest of Spain.

Major transformations occurred in the development, demography and society of the town. Terrassa expanded beyond its medieval structure towards Estació del Nord and, more importantly, by the early 20th century it had broken out of its traditional natural watercourse boundaries, Riera del Palau and Torrent de Vallparadís.

The usual idea of industrial heritage includes the most emblematic buildings where the industrial processes were actually carried out. In the case of the textile industry, this heritage comprises the chimneys, the steam-powered factories, the mills and the warehouses. Terrassa is the Catalan city where the largest number of items belonging to its textile industry heritage are still in existence. This concerns not just to the buildings recognised as being industrial as such, but also the development and creation of a town that grew out of a medieval structure, with everything that entails. All this can be

Terrassa

Address	Ajunatment de Terrassa - Tourist Office Raval de Montserrat, 14 08221 Terrassa
Opening hours and visits	Guided tours (previous booking required) every Saturday, except in December and from August 1st to September 15th. Tour starts at 10.30am from the Terrassa Tourist Office, and lasts approximately 3 hours
Information	Tel.: 937 397 019 and 937 336 369 Fax: 937 397 063 www.terrassa.org/turisme turisme@terrassa.org
Getting there	By train: FGC trains bound for Terrassa and Manresa, from Plaça de Catalunya station; RENFE trains bound for Manresa from Sants or Plaça Catalunya stations. By car: road C-58 (exit Terrassa-centre)
Further details	Check updates and information on Route discount at **www.rutadelmodernisme.com** or call 902 076 621

seen in the layout of the streets, in the number and location of the steam-powered factories, in the mills and warehouses, but also in the workers' dwellings -with all their different types and particular characteristics- and in the facilities set up to service industry and inhabitants, such as the railway station, the banks, the electricity supply, the hospital, the market, the hotels and the schools. It can even be seen in the spaces dedicated to supplying food and other services, or leisure and recreation, such as shops, chemists', tobacconists', fire stations, the casino, clubs, choral societies, cinemas and theatres. And it can also be seen in some of the items of street elements or the streets themselves with their cobblestones, pavements, lampposts, electrical items and carriage entrances.

Many of these industrial elements have survived in Terrassa to this day. Some of them are quite interesting taken separately, but overall they represent one of the most outstanding collections of industrial heritage in Catalonia.

Architectural Modernisme in Terrassa

Modernisme in architecture is generally characterised by the predominance of curved lines over straight lines -the use of parabolic and elliptical arches, the Catalan vault in the space between girders, and rounded edges-, the wealth and detail of the decoration, the frequent use of vegetable motifs and the dynamism of the shapes. The most commonly used materials are plain brickwork (although stucco and stone are also to be found), decorative ceramics, wrought iron and sgraffiti. These general features also apply to Terrassa, especially in the essentially practical and functional aspects of the use of the buildings. The exterior decorations are usually austere, whereas the interiors are finely decorated with ceramic banisters, leaded stained glass, woodwork and ironwork.

Pizzeria Restaurant Viena - Interior

The local exhibition at the Real Colegio Tarrasense in 1883 marked the start of the renovation of the plastic arts in Terrassa. This initial boost paved the way for the introduction of new artistic currents imported from Europe that arrived via Barcelona: Art Nouveau and the Modern Style. The highpoint of this new Modernista style in the town was the exhibition at Palau d'Indústries (now Escola Industrial) in 1904 with the applied arts particularly prominent. Local artist Joaquim Vancells and Alexandre de Riquer from Barcelona made a decisive contribution to the spread of Modernisme to painting and ornamentation in Terrassa.

However the extension and spread of this style in the city are due to the architects Lluís Muncunill and Josep M. Coll i Bacardí, and, to a lesser extent, Melcior Vinyals and Antoni Pascual i Carretero. It was these professionals, together with builders and craftsmen, who transformed the city with public buildings, factories, warehouses and private dwellings. This transformation occurred at the same time as the industrial development and the cultural and artistic concerns of the bourgeoisie of the moment. This style survived in Terrassa practically until the 1930s, beyond the limits usually attributed to the movement.

Outstanding among the early Art Nouveau works in Terrassa are the plans for the assembly hall of the **Industrial Institute**, with mural paintings by Alexandre de Riquer (1901) that were finished by Joaquim Vancells (1904) following a disagreement with the Institute. The decoration by Vancells remains in place and the central painting, by Riquer, is today in the dining room of Casa Alegre de Sagrera. The versatile Joaquim Vancells has also left us several projects in this style: the furniture in the dining room and office of **Masia Freixa**, the paintings on the stairs of **Casa Alegre de Sagrera** and the overall design of **Confiteria Vídua Carné**. The rooting of the Modernista style in Terrassa as applied to the town's industrial heritage is linked to the work of the most prolific local architect of the period: Lluís Muncunill.

The "Industrial and Modernista Terrassa" Route

This Route includes the town's 25 most representative buildings and monuments. Since they are all fairly close together, they can be visited on foot in half a day. The **former Vapor Aymerich**, Amat i Jover, once one of the most spectacular factories in Europe and now home to the Museum of Science and Technique of Catalonia, was designed by Lluís Muncunill (1907). It still has a very impressive 11,000 square metre bay, the engine room, the chimney and the old coal bunkers. This former steam-powered factory shows you what the world of the workers and industry was like at that time before going on to buildings that bring you closer to the daily life of the city and its bourgeoisie. Next you go down Rambla d'Ègara to **Mercat de la Independència** (1906), which has a metal structure and remarkable wrought iron decoration. Continuing along Raval de Montserrat you come to the former **Confiteria Carné,** originally a sweet shop, now a chemists' called Farmàcia

Industrial Institute

Albiñana, and an extraordinary example of Modernista decorative arts; the former headquarters of the **Societat General d'Electricitat** (now converted into a restaurant); the **Town Hall** (l'Ajuntament), a Neo-Gothic-style building (1903). The former **Industrial Institute** (now Centre Excursionista) and **Magatzem Cortès i Prat** (1897) are the most noteworthy buildings until you come to **Casa Alegre de Sagrera**. This building (dating from the early 19th century, but renovated in 1911 and now part of the Museum of Terrassa) was the residence of an old family of industrialists and is an example of an extremely eclectic Modernista style. The outstanding interior features include paintings by Joaquim Vancells i Pere Viver, woodwork, leaded stained glass and glass work, and the great Modernista paintings by Alexandre de Riquer in the dining room. A visit to **Gran Casino** (1920), a recently restored sumptuous building, is a must. On the way to the building and gardens of the **Industrial Institute** (the former Pasqual Sala store, 1893) you will see various houses that retain the spirit of the industrial Terrassa of a hundred years ago: **Casa Concepció Monset**, **Casa Baltasar Gorina** and **Cases de Cal Maurí** (a group of humble dwellings for workers, one of the few still remaining in Catalonia). The **Teatre Principal** is another landmark on the route through Modernista Terrassa. This is a monumental building erected in 1911 and now in disuse. Old stores and houses (**Magatzem Francesc Roig, Magatzem Emili Matalonga, Casa Jacint Bosch, Magatzem Joaquim Alegre, Magatzem Torras**, etc.) accompany you on your way to Carrer de la Rasa, where you will find the section of the **Ventalló factory**, which has been converted into a public space and a residential area including a square with arcades, the **Marcet i Poal factory** (1920) and **warehouse** (1914), and, finally, the section of the **Izard factory** (1921), a spectacular building that opens onto Plaça Didó and is now home to the Sala d'Exposicions Muncunill (Muncunill Exhibitions Hall) in what was once the factory's dyeing room. The route ends in the middle of Parc de Sant Jordi at **Masia Freixa** (1905-1910), the former residence and also factory of the Freixa family, designed by Lluís Muncunill.

Ajuntament de Terrassa
(Terrassa Town Council)

Modernisme in Vilafranca del Penedès

The economic resurgence of the Alt Penedès, after a plague of phylloxeras had destroyed the vineyards, the basis of the shire's economy, paved the way for the arrival of the artistic and social current that was beginning to take hold in Europe. Farm owners and merchants became the receivers of Modernista trends and had buildings put up in keeping with their economic position.

Towards the end of the 19th century, Vilafranca begun its transformation from a village into a small town as new buildings sprang up, changing its traditional image, and plans were laid for a new type of town. Renowned architects took over from master builders and there emerged the figures of Santiago Güell, Eugeni Campllonch and Antoni Pons. Santiago Güell (Vilafranca, 1869) was the municipal architect and played an active part in the political life of Vilafranca. As an architect he was scrupulous and a perfectionist. It was he who left the biggest imprint on the town, creating the

Lamps on Santa Maria Street

Ruta Modernista de Vilafranca del Penedès

Address	Tourist Office Cort, 14 08720 Vilafranca del Penedès
Opening hours and visits	Guided visits in downtown Vilafranca, including a Modernista music concert (homage to Apel·les Mestres): April through June and October through December, on the first Sunday of every month, starting at 11am. Visits last approximately 3 hours. Previous booking required. Privately booked visits are available all year round for groups of at least 8 people.
Information	Tel.: 938 181 254 Fax: 938 181 479 turisme@vilafranca.org www.turismevilafranca.com
Getting there	By train: RENFE trains bound for Sant Vicenç de Calders or Vilafranca itself, from Sants or Passeig de Gràcia stations. By bus: Hispano Igualadina company (tel.: 938 044 451) By road: toll highways AP2 and AP7 (exit 29), or road N-340
Further details	Check updates and information on Route discount at **www.rutadelmodernisme.com** or call 902 076 621

Casa Guardiet

Casa Cañas i Mañé

town's image and designing many of its most emblematic buildings. These buildings were characterised by mastery of the architectural technique and personal touches which he applied to his works with sobriety, elegance and balance.

Modernista architecture in Vilafranca combines popular Catalan architecture with the traits typical of Modernisme, which contributed new materials and a new conception of space. On the route through Modernista Vilafranca you will be able to see the colourful naturalistic decoration of the façades, the use of exposed brickwork on some buildings and the stained glass and wrought iron railings on windows and balconies.

Saint Mary's Basilica - Sculptural ensemble by Llimona

Vilafranca's Modernista heritage comprises 33 buildings of the most varied kinds: ancestral homes, public buildings and warehouses catering for the export of wines and liqueurs, clear exponents of the importance of industrial architecture in its own right.

Modernisme also embraced other aspects of art such as painting, sculpture and urban furniture design. As you walk along Carrer de Santa Maria, right in the centre of Vilafranca, you will see some singular examples of this latter type in the form of streetlamps. If you go into the Crypt of the Basilica you will find an excellent sculpture by Josep Llimona and in the Vilafranca Museum there are drawings by Ricard Opisso as well as works by other Modernista artists.

This Vilafranca route allows you to learn about the impact this cultural movement had at the turn of the century through the new symbols of progress and modernity contributed by the innovative trend called Modernisme.

Modernisme and music
Apel·les Mestres i Oñós (Barcelona 1854-1936)

Modernista music concerts

Making use of the scores in the musical archives of the Vilafranca Museum - Wine Museum, a considerable range of the music written by Apel·les Mestres has been recovered as it constitutes a representative example of Catalan Modernista music.

Apel·les Mestres's links with Vilafranca are significant due to his relationship with the local poet Lluís Via and the musician and folklorist Francesc de Paula Bové.

As a good Modernista, Apel·les Mestres was a versatile artist interested in taking an active part in culture and giving it new forms and contents. As a participant in the Modernista phenomenon, he was at one and the same time a poet, sketcher, composer, gardener and art collector. He set to music poems synthesising the Modernista ideals: the will for Catalonia to have a voice of its own in the world, Romanticism, nature as a force arising out of the earth and as a life force, and female beauty and an ironic way of looking at things as forms of human sensitivity.

Although he himself wrote a large number of songs that were frequently performed, achieved great popularity and today part of the repertoire of traditional Catalan songs, Apel·les Mestres never looked on himself as a composer, defining himself instead as a "songster". However his poetry was set to music by the best Catalan composers of the time including Enric Granados, Enric Morera and Joan Lamote de Grignon.

As a complement to the Vilafranca del Penedès Modernista route, a selection of music by Apel·les Mestres has been made containing popular and spontaneous elements and dealing with nature, the geographies of life and the beauty of the female in the imagination. A total of thirteen pieces taken from the musical archives of the Vilafranca Museum - Wine Museum, some of them never previously performed, make up the programme of this exclusive session of music that ends the guided tour of Modernista Vilafranca.

Patronat Municipal de Comerç i Turisme (Municipal Trade and Tourism Board)

Onomastic Index

Maps of Barcelona

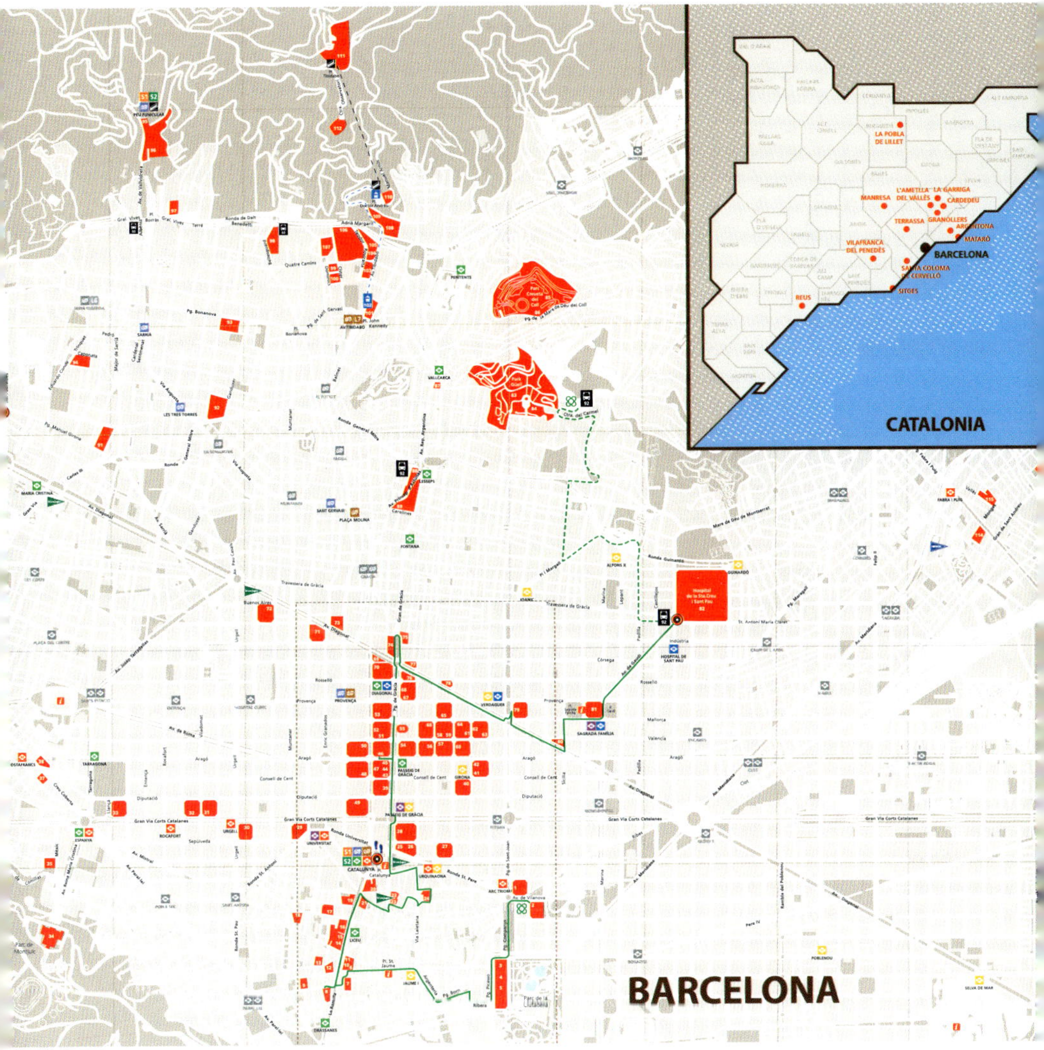

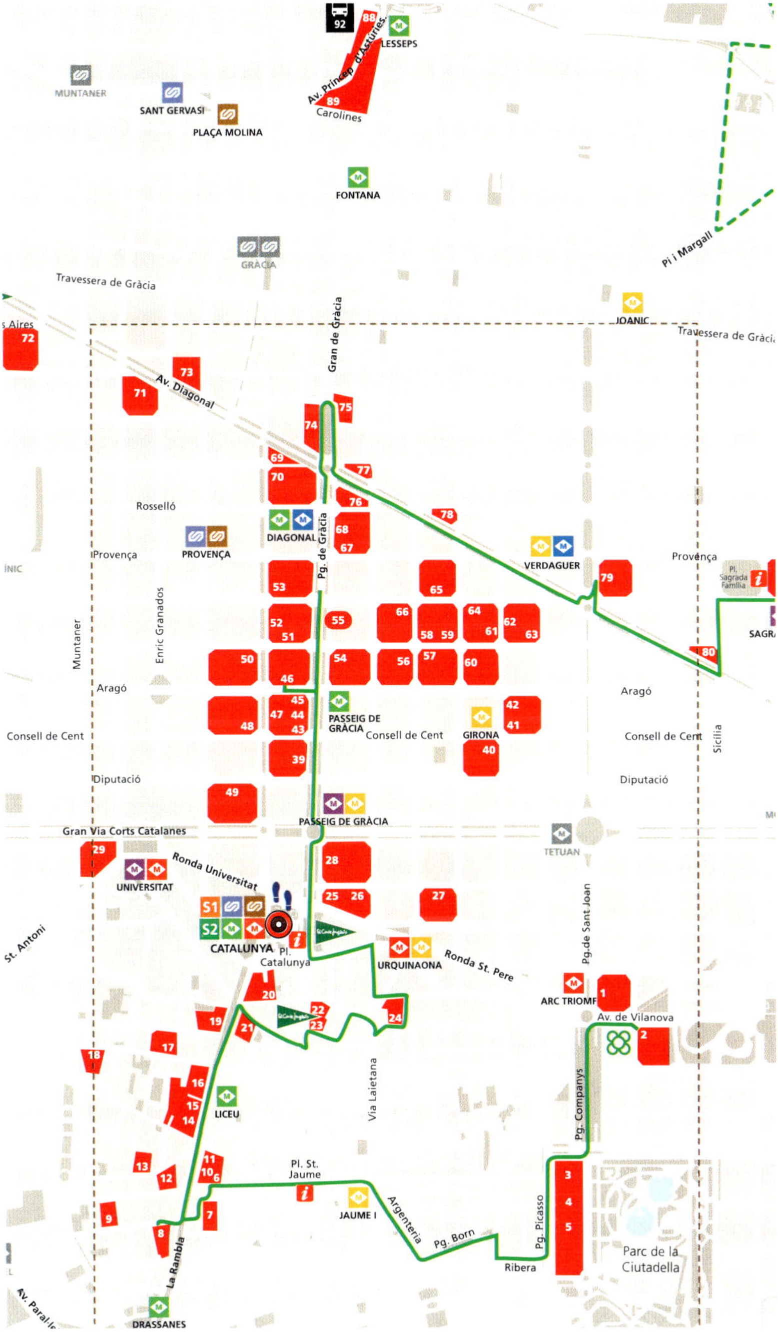

Modernisme Centre

1 29

39 80

88 89

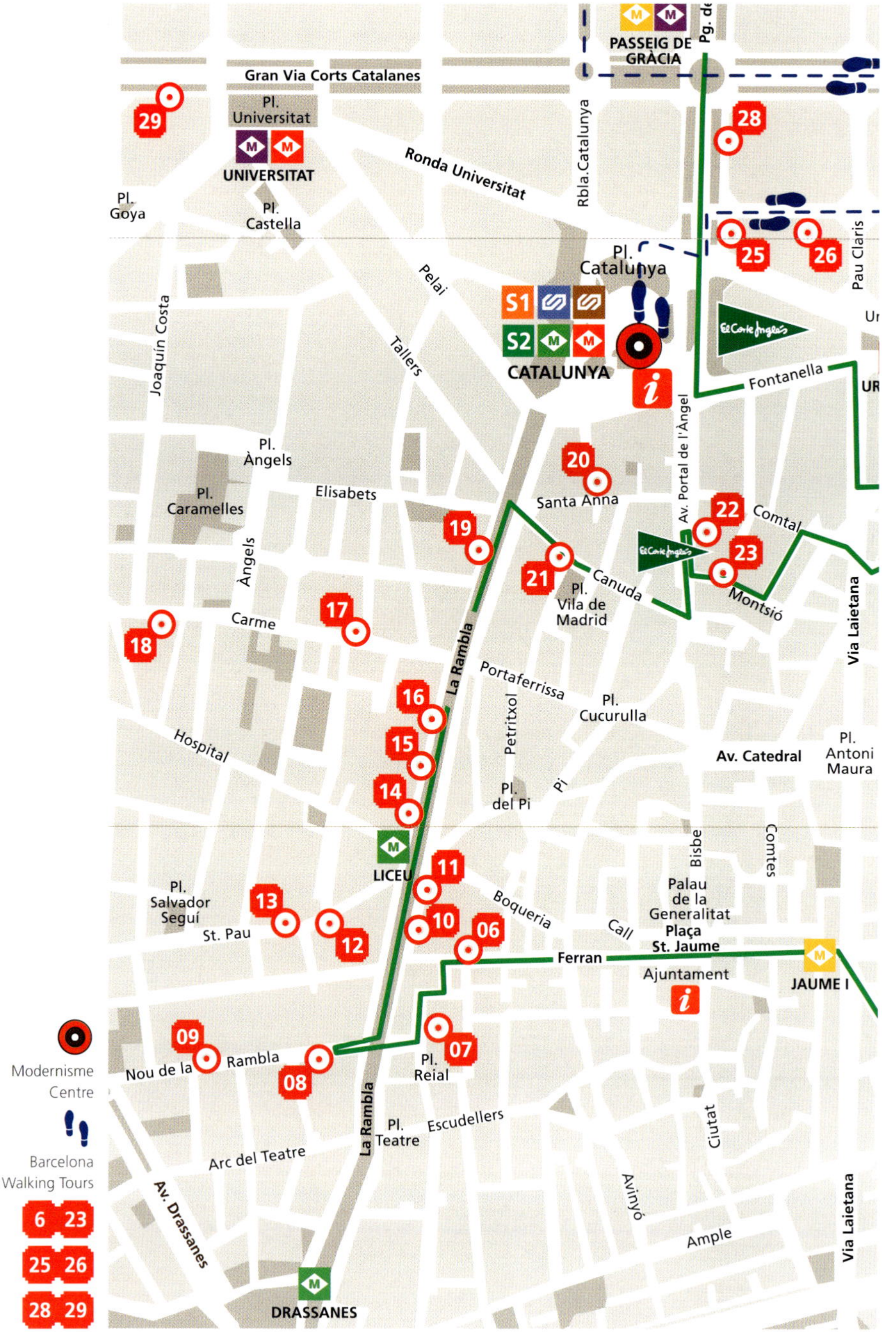

PASSEIG DE GRÀCIA
Pg. de
Gran Via Corts Catalanes
Pl. Universitat
UNIVERSITAT
Ronda Universitat
Rbla.Catalunya
Pl. Goya
Pl. Castella
Pl. Catalunya
Pau Claris
Pelai
S1
S2
CATALUNYA
Fontanella
Joaquín Costa
Tallers
Av. Portal de l'Àngel
Pl. Àngels
Elisabets
Santa Anna
Pl. Caramelles
Comtal
Àngels
Canuda
Pl. Vila de Madrid
Montsió
Carme
La Rambla
Portaferrissa
Via Laietana
Pl. Cucurulla
Petritxol
Hospital
Av. Catedral
Pl. Antoni Maura
Pl. del Pi
Pi
Bisbe
Comtes
LICEU
Pl. Salvador Seguí
Boqueria
Palau de la Generalitat
St. Pau
Call
Plaça St. Jaume
Ferran
Ajuntament
JAUME I
Nou de la Rambla
Pl. Reial
Pl. Teatre
Escudellers
Arc del Teatre
Ciutat
Av. Drassanes
Avinyó
Ample
DRASSANES
29 28 25 26 20 22 23 19 21 17 18 16 15 14 11 13 10 06 12 09 07 08
Modernisme Centre
Barcelona Walking Tours
6 23
25 26
28 29

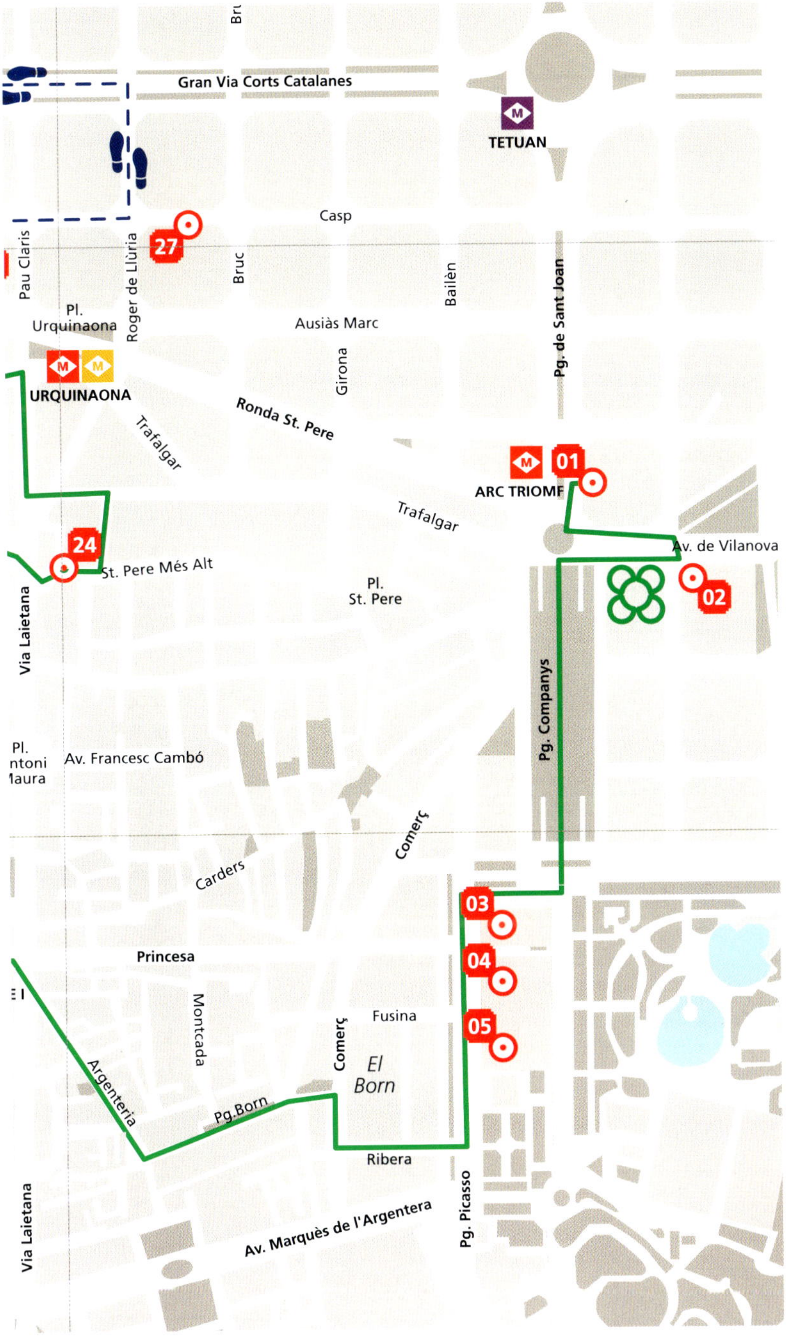
Gran Via Corts Catalanes
TETUAN
Casp
Pau Claris
27
Roger de Llùria
Bruc
Bailèn
Pg. de Sant Joan
Pl.
Urquinaona
Ausiàs Marc
Girona
URQUINAONA
Ronda St. Pere
Trafalgar
ARC TRIOMF
01
Trafalgar
Av. de Vilanova
24
St. Pere Més Alt
Pl.
St. Pere
02
Via Laietana
Pg. Companys
Av. Francesc Cambó
Comerç
Carders
03
Princesa
04
Montcada
Fusina
05
Comerç
El
Born
Argenteria
Pg.Born
Ribera
Pg. Picasso
Via Laietana
Av. Marquès de l'Argentera

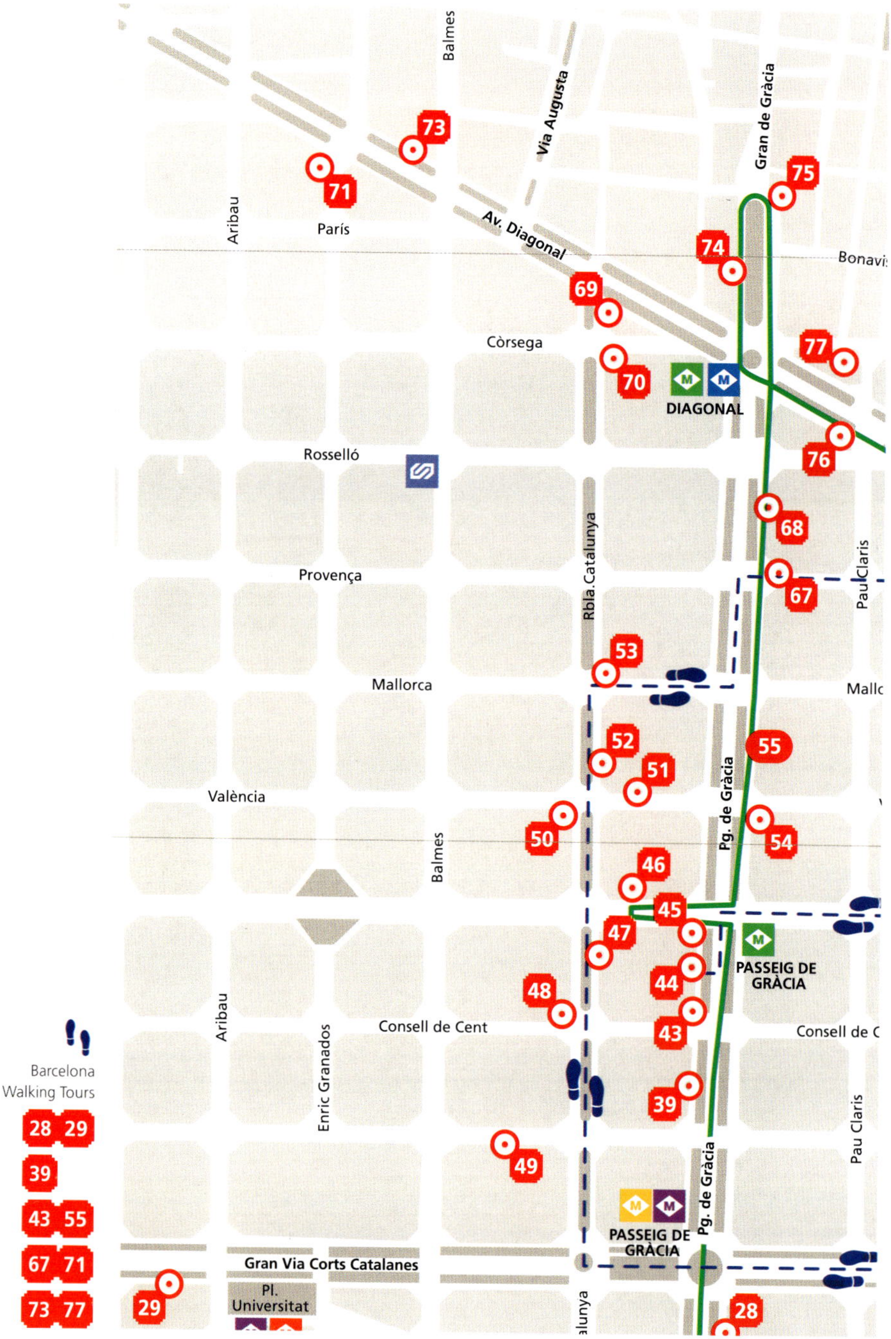

Balmes
Via Augusta
Gran de Gràcia
Aribau
París
Av. Diagonal
Bonavis
Còrsega
DIAGONAL
Rosselló
Provença
Rbla.Catalunya
Pau Claris
Mallorca
Mallo
València
Pg. de Gràcia
Balmes
PASSEIG DE GRÀCIA
Consell de Cent
Consell de C
Aribau
Enric Granados
Pau Claris
Pg. de Gràcia
PASSEIG DE GRÀCIA
Gran Via Corts Catalanes
Pl. Universitat
alunya
73 71 75 74 69 77 70 76 68 67 53 55 52 51 50 54 46 45 47 44 48 43 39 49 29 28
Barcelona Walking Tours
28 29
39
43 55
67 71
73 77

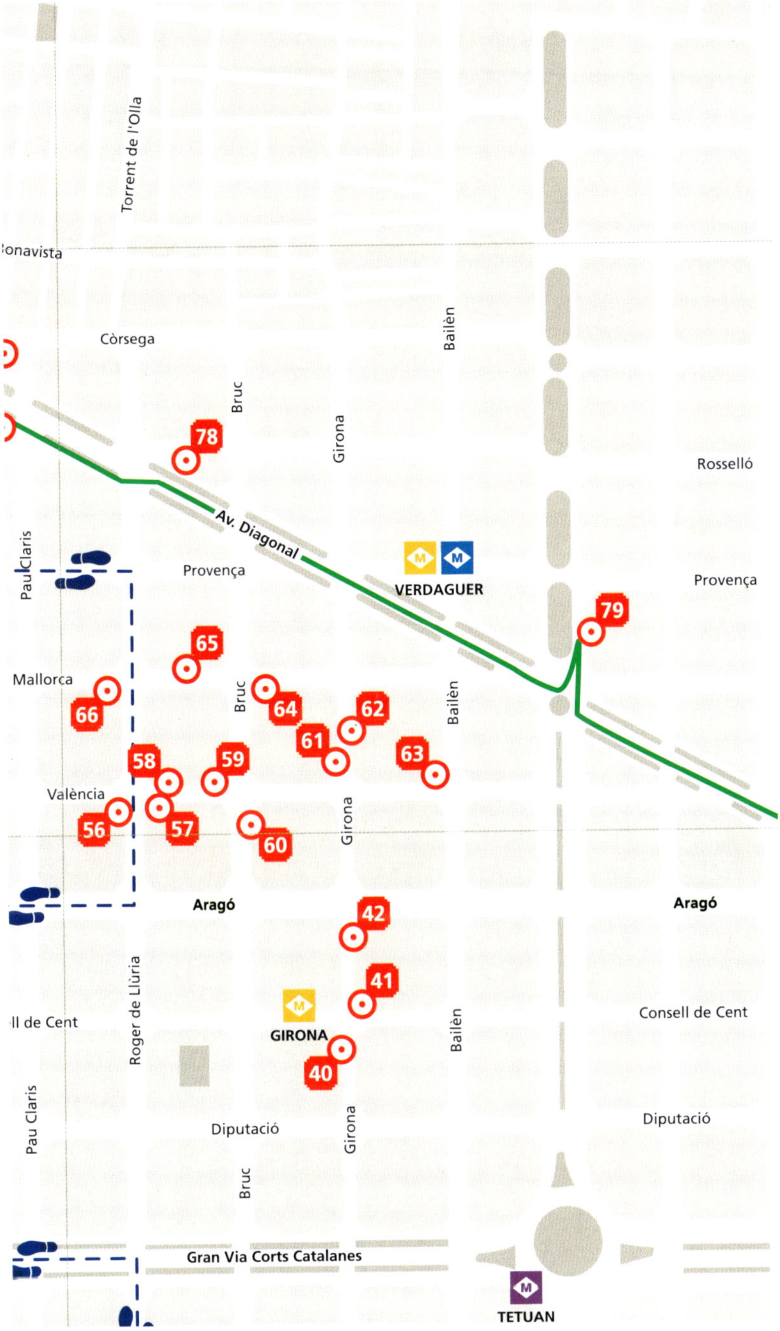

Barcelona Walking Tours

40 42
56 66
78 79

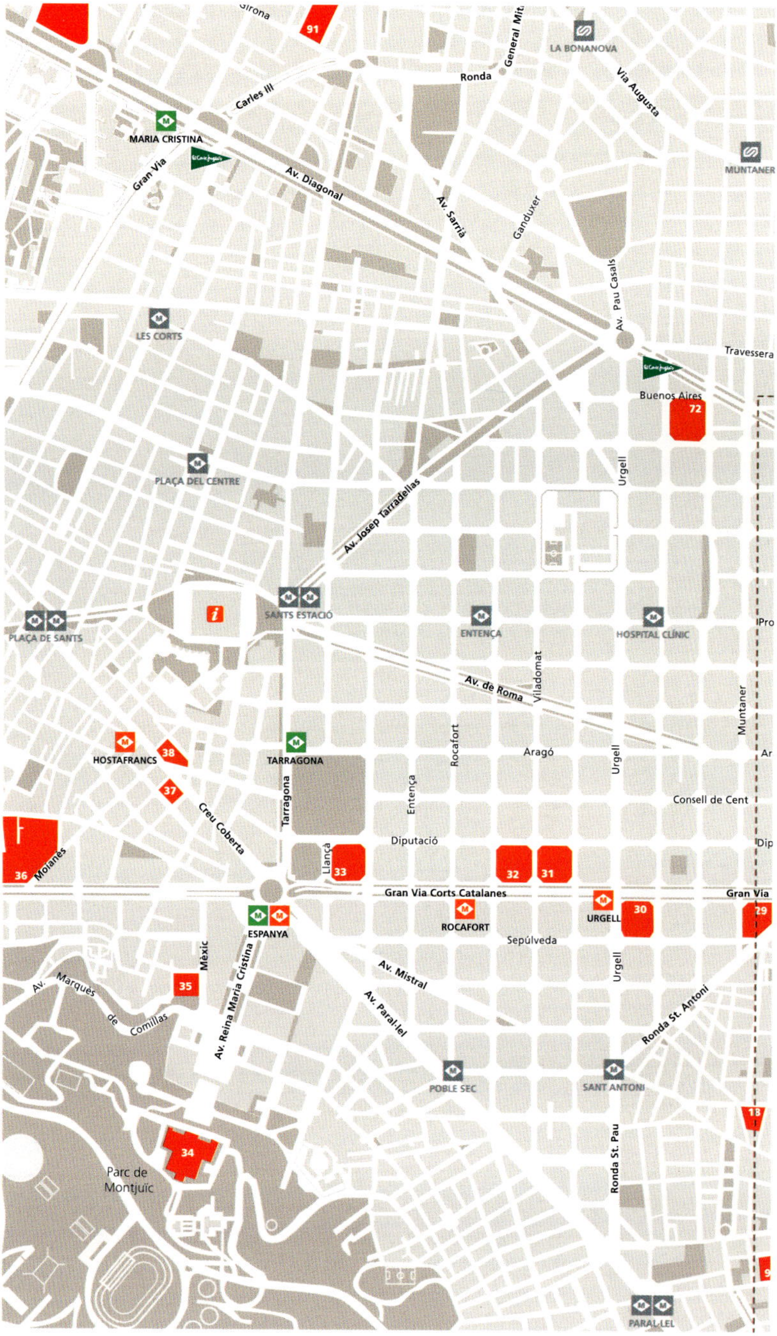

9
18
29 38
72
91

Modernisme Centre

1 5
24
27
40 42
56 66
78 82
88

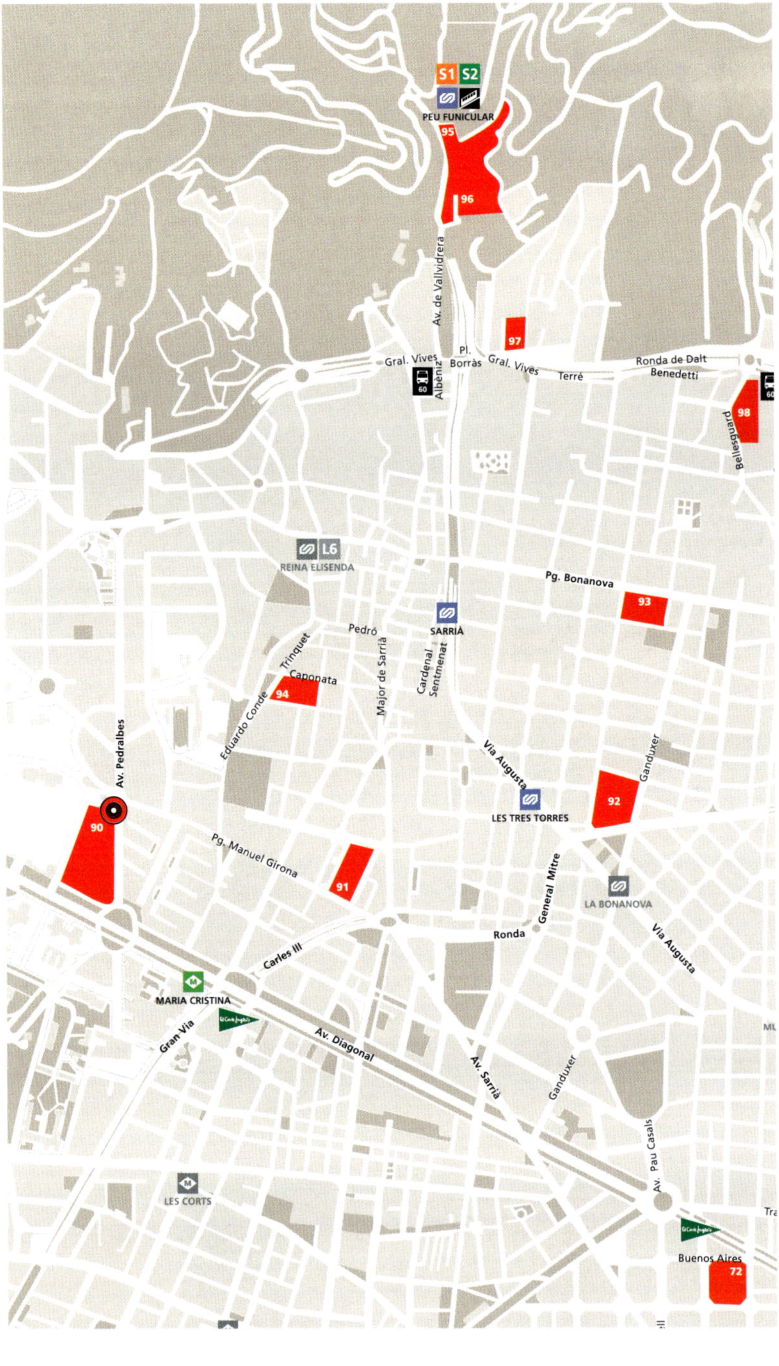

Modernisme Centre

72

90 98

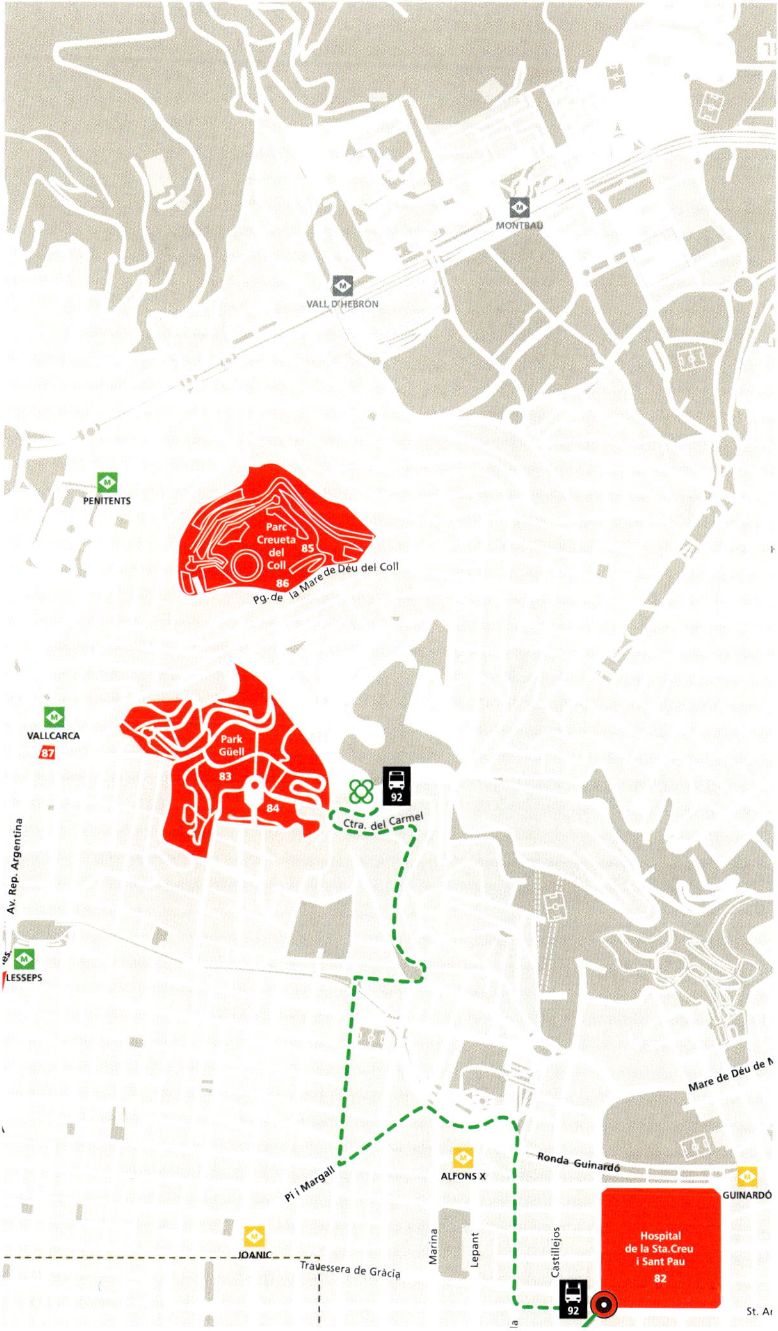

Modernisme Centre

82 87

111
Pl. Tibidabo
Ctra. Observatori
112
Manuel Arnús
110
Pl. Doctor Andreu
109
Adrià Margarit
108
60
98
Bellesguard
106
Teodor Roviralta
105
104
107
Quatre Camins
99
100
Dominics
Cister
103
Av. Tibidabo
102
101
L7
Pl. John Kennedy
AV.TIBIDABO
Pg. de Sant Gervasi
Pl. Bonanova
VALL D'HEBRON
PENITENTS
Parc Creueta del Coll
85
86
Pg. de la Mare de Déu del Coll
VALLCARCA
87
Park Güell
83
84
92
Ctra. del Carm
Balmes
EL PUTXET
Muntaner
Ronda General Mitre
Av. Rep. Argentina
PÀDUA
92
88
LESSEPS
Av. Príncep d'Astúries
89
Carolines
MUNTANER
SANT GERVASI
PLAÇA MOLINA
FONTANA
GRÀCIA
Pi i Margall
Travessera

LLUCMAJOR
VILAPICINA
VIRREI AMAT
Av. Meridiana
Pg. Fabra i Puig
113
MARAGALL
FABRA I PUIG
Vallès
115
SANT ANDREU
ntserrat
Monges
Gran de Sant Andreu
114
HIPERCOR
CONGRÉS
Felip II
Pg. Maragall
SAGRERA
oni Maria Claret
Av. Meridiana
AMP DE L'ARPA
NAVAS
BAC DE RODA
Gran Via Corts Catalanes
el Poblenou
de Prim

The discounts of the Barcelona Modernisme Route

The purchase of this guide already entitles you to the discounts of the Modernisme Route. **If you show this guide** at one of our **Modernisme Centres** we will give you the **book of discount vouchers for the Route**, allowing you to visit the main Modernista buildings of the city -and the local routes of thirteen other municipalities of Catalonia- at a reduced price. Discount vouchers are valid for one year from the moment you collect them.

You can also buy the rest of the Route pack at a special price. In addition to the discounts, it includes:

The map of the Barcelona Modernisme Route, with the 115 best Modernista works.
Let's Go Out, a guide to Modernista bars and restaurants.
The *Let's Go Out* map.
A genuine and convenient bag in which to keep everything while you visit the city.

The Barcelona City Council devotes all profits from the sales of the Barcelona Modernisme Route guide to the restoration and improvement of the Modernista heritage of the city.

Centre del Modernisme
Centre de Turisme de Barcelona
Pl. Catalunya, 17 basement
08002 Barcelona

Centre del Modernisme
Hospital de Sant Pau
C. Sant Antoni Maria Claret, 167
08025 Barcelona

Centre del Modernisme
Pavellons Güell
Av. de Pedralbes, 15
08034 Barcelona

www.rutadelmodernisme.com
E-mail: cultura-impuqv@mail.bcn.es
Tel.: (+34) 902 076 621

Space reserved for the stamp indicating withdrawal of the discount vouchers, which will be valid until: